SCAMMED

HOW TO SAVE YOUR MONEY
AND FIND BETTER SERVICE
in a **WORLD** *of*
SCHEMES,
SWINDLES,
AND SHADY DEALS

SCAMMED

CHRISTOPHER ELLIOTT

WILEY

John Wiley & Sons, Inc.

Published by John Wiley & Sons, Inc., Hoboken, New Jersey.

Published simultaneously in Canada.

For general information on our other products and services or for technical support, please contact our Customer Care Department within the United States at (800) 762-2974, outside the United States at (317) 572-3993 or fax (317) 572-4002.

Wiley publishes in a variety of print and electronic formats and by print-on-demand. Some material included with standard print versions of this book may not be included in e-books or in print-on-demand. If this book refers to media such as a CD or DVD that is not included in the version you purchased, you may download this material at **http://booksupport.wiley.com**. For more information about Wiley products, visit **www.wiley.com**.

Library of Congress Cataloging-in-Publication Data:

Elliott, Christopher, 1968–
   Scammed: how to save your money and find better service in a world of schemes, swindles, and shady deals/Christopher Elliott.
      p. cm.
   Includes bibliographical references.
   ISBN 978-1-118-10800-0 (hardback: acid-free paper); ISBN 978-1-118-18015-0 (ebk); ISBN 978-1-118-18014-3 (ebk); ISBN 978-1-118-18013-6 (ebk)
   1. Fraud—United States.   2. Swindlers and swindling—United States.   3. Computer crimes—United States.   4. Corporations—United States—Public opinion.   5. Social responsibility of business—United States.   1. Title.
"HV6695.E37 2011
332.024—dc23   2011032040

Printed in the United States of America.

10 9 8 7 6 5 4 3 2 1

For the victims.

Contents

Prologue
Fenced In

The easiest person to deceive is one's self.

—Edward Bulwer-Lytton

OCEANA DRIVE IS a quiet road in a Key Largo, Florida, neighborhood that dead-ends into the Atlantic. In 2002, just after our first son was born, most of the lots along the street were overgrown with sabal palms and gumbo limbo trees. Our modest two-bedroom house backed up against a busier subdivision, but if you looked out the window of our living room, you'd think we lived in a jungle.

Well, most of the time.

During spring break, drunken vacationers would amble through our yard after hours, hoping to find a shortcut to the housing development behind us. Our only neighbors had an annoying habit of parking their trailer on our property. At the end of the street, the residents of a coral rock castle often confused Oceana for a drag-racing track, zooming past our home in their convertibles. By the time our son Aren was taking his first steps, it became abundantly clear: we needed a fence.

I soon found myself writing a $400 check to an unlicensed contractor "for supplies." I didn't hesitate. He'd been endorsed by friends, and his rates were affordable. A few days later, he knocked on our front door, dropped off a small truckload of lumber, and dug a few holes for the fence posts.

Then he disappeared.

"Have you heard from him?" we asked our friends, after he stopped answering his phone. Yes, they said. He had to go "up north" for a family emergency, and ours wasn't the only project he'd left undone.

We never saw him again.

We'd been scammed.

Remember the last time someone pulled a fast one on you? "I should have seen that one coming," you said, kicking yourself. I certainly did after our experience with the fence guy. And I was right. I *should* have.

If it happened to you, would you dismiss it as a momentary lapse in judgment? I did at the time.

But I was wrong. Consumers have been conditioned to fall for bogus offers, and not just the seemingly obvious ones. In recent years, they've even become complicit in many of the everyday and often perfectly legal raids on their wallets that await in innocent places, from the mall to the supermarket.

In other words, I'm part of the problem, and so are you. And it's a *big* problem.

Scams are shockingly common, ranging from a sneaky $25 overdraft fee to investment frauds that can suck hundreds of thousands of dollars from your bank account.

Tens, maybe hundreds, of millions of Americans are scammed every year, in large and small ways. You've probably been one of them. You may be one now. The Federal Trade Commission received more than one million complaints from the public in 2010, most of them about alleged rip-offs.

Consumer Complaints

Year	Number
2007	1,050,383
2008	1,224,995
2009	1,330,426
2010	1,339,265

Source: Federal Trade Commission.

A breakdown of these complaint categories reads like a twenty-first-century rap sheet for the aspiring criminal: identity theft, Internet swindles, phony sweepstakes, virtual auctions that leave you poorer but wiser, and impostor scams. Those are just the ones that are discovered and reported. Many other questionable business practices go unnoticed by customers, and the damage from those swindles is probably far greater.

It's easy to point the finger at small-time fraudsters like a fence contractor and say: "Scam!"

It's not as easy when there's a legitimate company behind a questionable product or service. And it's all but impossible for us to accept that as customers, we're not only letting these predators victimize us, but actually *helping* them do so. But it's true, nonetheless.

Let's explore the ways in which countless businesses—from the largest multinational corporation, to the mom-and-pop store around the corner, to the independent contractor who does odd jobs—have developed new and sophisticated ways of taking you to the dry cleaners. I'll show you how consumers just like you have unwittingly encouraged them to do it (and you might find this hard to believe, even aided in the crime) and how you can break that cycle once and for all. I'll also offer strategies to help you spot the scams and save the money that might otherwise be lost.

The Key Largo fence fiasco wasn't the first time I've been scammed, nor was it the last. As a know-it-all senior in college, I lost $3,000 in a slick pyramid scheme. I've been ripped off by a pet store, a bed-and-breakfast, and a man on the street selling "new" TVs still in the box. Some of my best-known failings have been as a journalist, believing unscrupulous sources with too-good-to-be-true stories that ended up being half-true, and in some cases, not true at all. I felt betrayed each time, but I also came to learn that if I put certain safeguards in place, I could spare myself future embarrassments.

Although I never got my money back from the fence contractor, I later learned that he'd been arrested for other offenses. I consider the lost $400 to be a form of tuition. In a small but important way, he taught me how to be a better consumer.

I've written this book to teach you how to readjust your expectations. It's a call to arms for consumers everywhere to fight back—but more importantly, a practical guide on how to do that. And lucky for you, it costs a lot less than $400.

For example, did you even know you could file a grievance with the Feds for most transgressions against your pocketbook? Most people don't. (Turn to the Appendix for a list of agencies you can complain to when you're in trouble.) Problems sent to a government agency typically represent a small fraction of actual complaints—maybe 1 or 2 percent. That means at least 1 in 30 Americans is a victim of a scheme, swindle, or shady deal *every* year.

The good news: If you're smart about looking for the danger signals and quick to act if you do get cheated out of your hard-won cash, you can keep the con artists and legal wheeler-dealers at bay.

A Guide to *Scammed*

You can access this book in several different ways. You can read through it in sequential order, or you can page right to the section you're interested in. Here's what you need to know.

- A *box* (like this one) is an aside, usually an anecdote that illustrates the section's main point.
- The *charts and graphs* (like the one on consumer complaints in this chapter) offer a visual representation of the issue at hand. Sometimes, it's better to show than tell. Besides, the last thing I want to do is lecture.

Finally, you'll notice two regular features: *How to Save Money* and *How to Find Better Service*. Those are short tips on how to put what you've learned into action. Why? Because that's what this book is all about.

Scammed—or Just a Bad Deal?

Not every negative customer experience is a scam, of course. But *taken advantage of* doesn't have quite the ring of *scammed*. Consumers tend to use the terms *scam*, *rip-off*, and *bad deal* almost interchangeably—

just as we think of *steal, bargain,* and *good deal* as synonyms. But drawing a distinction is important.

Let's break it down.

Are You Being Served?

CASES WHERE THE COMPANY WINS

- *Scam.* A company that fraudulently misrepresents a product is trying to scam you or deprive you of your money by deceit. A scam is often accompanied by terms so restrictive that you don't have any recourse when you want to return the defective product.
- *Rip-off.* A lesser version of the scam, a rip-off can involve deception. However, it's usually not a company-wide practice. For example, a shady used-car dealership may rip you off by selling cars with their odometers rolled back, whereas a factory-authorized dealership might try to sell you an extended warranty for three times its actual worth.
- *Bad deal.* Every business marks its items up, and sometimes they overprice them or sell items that are of inferior quality. These are simply bad deals that can be avoided by shopping around. They are not fraudulent or even questionable. In fact, from a company's point of view, they're a good deal because their profit margins are significantly higher.

CASES WHERE THE CONSUMER WINS

- *Good deal.* This is the flip side of the bad deal. If an item is on sale or marked down from its original price, then the company makes less—or loses—money, but the customer has the upper hand. A good deal doesn't always involve a lower price. For example, if a company runs out of base models and offers you an upgraded model at no additional cost, that's a good deal.
- *Bargain.* A step beyond a good deal, the bargain is almost too good to be true. There are various subsets of bargains, from

(continued)

(*continued*)

selling distressed inventory to a going out of business sale, where every item is priced to move quickly. The company is almost certainly losing money in the transaction, unless it's one of those camera stores in Times Square that's been going out of business for the last 50 years.

■ *Steal.* This is the rough equivalent of the scam, except that the one being scammed in this case is the company. Believe it or not, customers can fraudulently take advantage of a company in any number of ways with a steal—and it doesn't have to involve shoplifting. Switching price tags or shorting a cash register through deception when you pay, are two popular scams used by consumers. It's a "win" for that customer—that is, until they're caught and hauled off to jail.

There's a line between "Consumer Wins" and "Company Wins." That's where business *should* take place—and it is a thin line. Sometimes businesses have the advantage, sometimes customers do. But the closer we are to the line, the better it is for everyone. Balance is good. Businesses thrive, and their customers are happy. When you move too far in one direction or another, you're courting disaster. At one end, there's the threat of recessions and business failures, and at the other, there are deeply cynical consumers who distrust companies and industries.

Unfortunately, the relationship between companies and customers is as dysfunctional nowadays as it's ever been.

As you'll soon see, the worst kinds of scams aren't the ones where you realize you've been hoodwinked. Those are largely the provenance of amateurs, snake-oil salesmen, and ethically challenged small businesses. I refer to these as *lowercase scams*. Much worse are the scams that are never detected because they're executed by professionals with MBAs and shattered moral compasses. I call these *uppercase scams*.

A majority of the books about scams and consumerism spend pages upon pages describing how to chase the lowercase scams—

finding the unscrupulous businesses, fixing the deals gone wrong, and preventing them from happening again. I'll do some of that in this book, too. But my primary focus will be on the scams that cost us untold billions a year: the uppercase scams that we're largely unaware of.

Isn't Everyone Running a Scam?

In a broad sense—a *very* broad sense—every business is running a scam of sorts. They take products that are cheap or free to them, repackage them, mark them up, sell them to you—and then pocket the difference. And sometimes the difference in price is so ridiculously big that it allows them to buy the mansion *and* the yacht.

If you stop to think about the way capitalism works, you might find yourself saying, "Hey, that's a scam!" (And in fact, many idealistic college freshmen do when introduced to other political philosophies. But I digress.) It's important to recognize that from a certain perspective, the relationship between a business and a customer will never appear *entirely* fair. And although we shouldn't expect life to always be fair, we have a right to demand that companies who profit from us will *treat* us fairly—and with respect—*all* the time. Even in capitalism, there's a difference between turning a profit and gouging the customer.

Down That Road Lies Madness

The relationship between businesses and consumers is broken almost beyond repair.

Businesses don't trust their customers. About three-quarters of all consumer contracts contain arbitration clauses that limit your ability to sue a company. Instead, you have to use the services of a professional arbitrator, who often favors the corporation. Most consumers don't know they've agreed to the terms merely by opening the packaging.

Some companies have even successfully lobbied the government to limit your ability to sue them. For instance, the airline and cruise industries impose strict venue and time limits for lawsuits. You can't just walk down to your local courthouse and sue a cruise line whenever you want. You have a limited window of time to find a lawyer who understands admiralty law and will argue your case in a maritime court where your complaint also needs to be filed. The business community would like more, not fewer, limits on litigation; that way, they'd be protected even if their customers *did* have a case against them.

Instead of fighting these unfair clauses, consumers just steal. A 2011 survey by the Consumer Travel Alliance found that 28 percent of hotel guests would lie for a discount. British researchers Kate Reynolds and Lloyd Harris had little trouble recruiting more than 100 customers who had knowingly made a false complaint for their 2005 study. Among the most disturbing category of whiners are the professional complainants who lie for profit.

Stealing the Store

WORLDWIDE INVENTORY SHRINKAGE

2010	$107.3
2009	$114.8
2008	$104.5
2007	$.986

(Retail shrinkage is a broad term defined as a company's stock loss from crime or waste expressed as a percentage of retail sales.)

Source: Retail shrinkage from global theft in billions US$.

Consumers stole $107.3 billion in goods worldwide in 2010. Though this figure may have been off slightly due to the recession, it still represented more than 1 percent of total retail sales. For a big-box retailer like Wal-Mart, that can add up to an eye-popping $3 billion annually, give or take a few hundred million.

At the same time, the rhetoric from those advocating for consumers is hardening, urging customers to see the world as a conflict between us and them. While sometimes justified, this attitude can encourage reckless and even fraudulent consumer behavior. Indeed, some of the most popular voices pushing for consumer rights often sound like battle cries to take down every business. As one of my college professors liked to say: Down that road lies madness.

It isn't difficult to imagine what the world might look like if this destructive downward spiral isn't stopped. As the corporate rip-offs and bait-and-switch schemes get smarter, customers strike back by stealing and swindling. Mutual distrust grows. Sure, other forces, like the economy and basic human psychology, are at work here. But there's little doubt that the deteriorating relationship between companies and customers is driving us into an abyss.

Is it any wonder that consumers as a group feel there's no hope? Their perceived victimization is one of the themes of Guy Winch's 2011 book, *The Squeaky Wheel: Get Results, Improve Your Relationships, Enhance Your Self-Esteem*. As the title suggests, customers' belief that businesses are out to get them can have a profound effect on their self-esteem and indeed, their overall happiness.

Companies think their customers are liars and thieves. Customers believe they have a target painted on their backs. That's some pickle we've gotten ourselves into.

Thankfully, there's a way out.

Introduction
You're Not a Victim

Never give in except to convictions of honor and good sense.
—Winston Churchill

THE MOST CHALLENGING part of being a consumer advocate isn't battling unyielding companies (of which there are plenty) or enduring long, thankless hours staring at a computer screen (ditto). It's handling the inbred defeatism of most consumers. Just today, I got an e-mail from a reader that began, "Dear Chris, you probably won't respond to this, just as the company I'm dealing with hasn't responded to me. I guess I'm out of luck." No luck here. I shot back a reply within seconds: "Sorry to disappoint you."

It's not surprising that we cast ourselves as the helpless targets of predators. The double dealers who have ripped us off are often deep-pocketed corporations able to hide behind impenetrable barriers of automatic phone systems, or else they are anonymous tricksters whose identities elude us.

But that's the absolute *wrong* way of seeing things.

We can avoid the traps. And if we do get ensnared, we can fight back. But we have to change the way we think and ultimately become contrarians instead of cattle in a herd or lemmings being led unknowingly off a cliff.

For example, research conducted in 2004 at Carnegie-Mellon University concluded that computer users could be taught to think differently about certain scams. The study focused on phishing, or the act of fraudulently trying to acquire passwords and other personal information. After playing a game, many participants were less likely to fall for a simulated phishing attack. It proves you *can* control that desire to buy something that's a bad deal or resist the irrational pull of a clever scam.

Study after case study supports this premise that enlightened buyers are better customers.

Companies should love these smart consumers because they're more likely to buy their products, if their products are any good. However, educating customers can be expensive and requires a long-term view, which is a rarity in a business environment that is fixated on today's stock price.

Corporations are likely to try and make a quick buck at your expense but you don't have to play the dupe. If you keep alert and follow a few simple guidelines, you'll stay in control of your wallet.

Confessions of a Heretic

Of course, the idea that consumers run the show isn't a new one. Anyone who passed Economics 101 can connect the dots and figure out that the people doing the buying are the ones calling the shots. The notion that you're part of the scam problem, however, is heresy to some consumer advocates.

As it turns out, I'm totally into heresy.

I have a personal reason for sticking it to the folks who are sticking it to us. Members of my family have been victimized by cons that cheated them out of thousands of dollars. The swindlers spare no one. Quite the contrary, they prey on the elderly and the uneducated because they are their most gullible targets.

My 93-year-old grandmother in Southern California is hammered with bogus investment offers and you-may-already-be-a-millionaire flyers in the mail five days a week. They also phone her at dinnertime, even though she's a charter member of the Do Not Call registry. At her grandson's insistence, she now tosses the Publisher Clearing House letters in the recycler and promptly hangs up on telemarketers.

I run a wiki called On Your Side (www.onyoursi.de) that explores the broken relationship between companies and their customers. You'll find the names, numbers, and addresses of the CEOs and VPs of every major American corporation on it.

Many executives consider their e-mail addresses and phone numbers to be proprietary. Unfortunately, they don't treat your personal information with the same care as their own, and instead they offer it to advertising "partners" the way a street preacher hands out tracts. The fact is, information must be freely available in a free market economy—and executives have to be held accountable.

I've been a journalist my entire career, starting with my first internship at the weekly *Claremont* (California) *Courier* in 1987. You can learn a lot about reporting at a community newspaper. You quickly realize that a public forum is too valuable to waste on simply regurgitating the week's news. You see that you can actually make the world a better place if you cover the right story in the right way—a lesson I learned well at Berkeley's journalism school.

I'm not quite sure when I went from being a reporter to a consumer advocate, but it probably happened many years before I would admit it. I pursued any story that could improve the life of ordinary readers. My work led directly to the introduction and passage of new laws, pushed companies to change their business practices, and secured refunds that totaled millions of dollars to aggrieved customers.

As you might imagine, it wasn't always easy. I've had some spectacular setbacks along the way. For example, I once reported that an airframe manufacturer was marketing standing-room seats on its aircraft, which proved to be not entirely correct (the seats were real, but the program had been abandoned a few years before). I wrote a story that the Federal Aviation Administration was allowing wireless devices to be used on aircraft (a misunderstanding with a government spokesman). I was even served with a subpoena by the Department of Homeland Security for publishing an unclassified document on my blog (the demand to name my source was dropped 48 hours later). And I was unsuccessfully sued for defamation by an angry travel agency owner.

I am not sorry for any of those things. On the contrary, I'm grateful. The lessons I learned from my mistakes are irreplaceable. Fighting subpoenas and frivolous litigation only made me more determined to help others.

I'm not perfect, and chances are that you'll find something to critique in this book. That's fine. I didn't choose this line of work because it was easy. I could have a cushy nine-to-five reporting job at any news organization, with benefits and paid holidays, but I'd rather be in the trenches fighting on the side of the people.

So, while I'm at it, let me make a few more treasonous statements.

- *The customer isn't always right and certainly is not "king."* Sometimes consumers do stupid, irrational things, often have no idea what they want, and then try to shame companies into doing their bidding. I know—because I've seen it happen.
- *Journalism is an imperfect tool.* It's not a religion—in spite of what my well-meaning colleagues seem to think. This book is a means to an end: I want to improve the customer experience. Period. If you are looking for "fair and balanced," well, you know where to go.
- *Some companies* really *do no evil.* I'm not about to suggest that *that* company does no evil—you know which one I'm talking about— but I can say this with some certainty: corporations are not uniformly predatory institutions. Even at some of the most customer-service–challenged businesses you will find people who care.

I can't tell you the story of how we are being scammed without offering these opinions. Without these heretical beliefs there would be no book, and I would be safely editing the Obituaries page at a newspaper and counting the years until I collect Social Security. (Maybe I'd sneak in an occasional exposé about mortuary scams; it is in my blood.)

But that's not who I am. And if you're reading this book, it's not you either.

Preventive Medicine

These are the facts: You are neither the victim of a faceless corporation nor of your own base desires. Rather, you're in control from the moment you get in the car or log on to your PC until the second you reach for your purse or click the Purchase button.

You are responsible.

But it's still a dangerous world for consumers. One of the first rules of Corporation 101 is to try to gain the upper hand against you.

In order to solve the problem, let us consider a topic that affects us in one way or another: namely, death.

Leading Preventable Causes of Death in America

Cause of Death	Deaths per Year
Tobacco	435,000
Poor diet and physical inactivity	400,000
Alcohol consumption	85,000
Microbial agents	75,000
Toxic agents	55 000
Motor vehicle crashes	43,000
Incidents involving firearms	29,000
Sexual behaviors	20,000
Illicit use of drugs	17,000

Source: Journal of the American Medical Association (2000).

Notice anything? No? Look again and you'll see almost all these deaths could have been prevented if the victims had gone into smoking cessation, followed a healthier diet, joined Alcoholics Anonymous, stuck to the speed limit or *just taken some initiative*.

Think of *Scammed* as preventive medicine. Each section will not only enlighten you to nascent challenges of the twenty-first-century customer but inoculate you against your own destructive (indeed, *self-destructive*) behavior.

How Businesses Are Scamming Us

Every day, corporations develop new and sophisticated ways of separating us from our money. In Part One, I dissect this creature that preys on you, often in your own home. This is no ordinary villain. It is a clever shape shifter that adapts to ever-evolving consumer behavior. The only way to outwit it is to learn to think like it, as opposed to adopting a bunch of formula solutions written up in bullet points. Not that there's anything wrong with bullet points. You see, businesses are smart and nimble. They learn.

I expose in these pages corporate lies, including the seductive ads, the deceitful fine print, and the customer testimonials that are littering the Internet, and demonstrate how you can use that knowledge to become the enlightened consumer ("Eat, Love, Shop"?) who will never be taken advantage of again. I also give a few hints about how companies must change their errant ways if they want to stay in business.

How We Are Letting Them

Unfortunately, these bad businesses get help from the unlikeliest of sources—you. Today's consumers don't bother to read the fine print; they never do their homework; and hardly think to ask the right questions. I explore why this is happening and show you how you can become a smarter consumer who can save lots of money in a few quick steps. I help you extricate yourself from the hypnotic technology that keeps valuable information out of your reach. I teach you how to *effectively* use the tools that can help you become a more informed consumer. And I tell you just who you can trust.

I also show you how to start thinking differently about the frayed relationship between companies and consumers, and how jettisoning the clichéd worldview—of meaningless terms like *us against them* or *winners* and *losers*—will make your consumer experience fairer and more profitable for everyone.

Is There a Virtuous Company?

The term *virtuous company* was popularized by Theodore Malloch's *Doing Virtuous Business: The Remarkable Success of Spiritual Enterprise*—a book that in 2008 argued how a deepened sense of spirituality could benefit corporate America. As the son of a

Protestant minister, I probably should steer clear of theology. But the idea that a company could be virtuous—or perhaps simply not evil—is an attractive one to any employee or manager reading this.

How do you tell if you're dealing with a virtuous company? Here's a short checklist:

- Employee morale and retention are high.
- People are promoted—not demoted—into customer-service positions. (You can often tell this happens when a company issues a press release on its newest customer-service VP.)
- There is generous profit sharing and a 401k matching program in place.
- The company donates a higher-than-average percentage of its profits to charity.
- It has a generous leave policy for sabbaticals or family needs.
- A business invests in employee training and enrichment programs, even when not required by law.

What to Do about It

No doubt about it; every day more people are being scammed in the most creative manners imaginable. And there's even more trouble ahead.

I'm not basing such a prophecy on the outrages of the recent past, such as the Wall Street bailouts and the highway robberies perpetrated against the little guy by corporate rodents like Enron. The sad fact is that the future looks no better.

It isn't that our regulators didn't learn the lessons of the recent past, or that lobbyists found ways to gut new rules meant to protect consumers before these were voted into law. It's that the global business community doesn't see any problem with its behavior.

Consider tomorrow's managers and CEOs, those much-ballyhooed students enrolled in MBA programs at elite business schools. A 2007 survey of the top 50 business schools by the *Financial Times* found that only a quarter required (or took) an ethics class. Granted, it was a five-fold increase from 1999, but still—it means 75 percent of tomorrow's business leaders have no formal ethics training. Have a look at the table below.

Have You Ever Cheated on an Exam? Percentage Who Said "Yes"

Business students	56%
Engineering students	54%
Education students	48%
Law students	45%

Source: Donald McCabe, Rutgers Business School (2008).

To say that some companies have no conscience and that they're nothing more than soulless moneymaking machines could be an exaggeration. But not much of one. When it comes to ethics and morality, we instinctively know better than to look to the captains of industry for guidance. So why do we act surprised when any company rips us off?

The New Scams

Today's businesses have developed a three-pronged approach to parting us from our cash.

1. *Lying about themselves*. Companies aren't just bending and stretching the truth in ads. They're also engaging in an emerging practice called Reputation Management designed to spiff up their corporate image. Ah, public relations—a force to be reckoned with in the corporate world. There is one reason, and only one, that they do this: these half-truths and spin turn you into a panting customer.
2. *Lying about their products*. Exaggerated product claims have been around since the cavemen traded clubs. But today's hype goes

further, often misrepresenting the price, the terms of the purchase, and what's in the box. Again, bogus claims make customers
of us all.

3. *Lying about your rights.* Companies bury surprise clauses that re-
strict you from legal relief in the fine print of their contracts and
terms. They push governments to limit customers' rights and
leave them holding all the cards. Although corporations make
warranties and guarantees, a close look at many of them reveals
that they aren't worth the paper they're printed on. However,
these assurances make us feel better about our purchases—and
therefore more likely to buy a product or service.

Many of today's companies are simply incapable of telling the
truth. In the next section, I tell you exactly how they try to distort
reality and I show you how you can spot their shenanigans and become an enlightened consumer who will never be ripped off again.

PART

How They Scam Us

1

Reputation Management

And listen, if you can't say anything real nice it's better not to talk at all, is my advice.

—Dean Martin

OH, THE LENGTHS to which companies go to protect their good name. They seem boundless. I remember mediating one reader's refund case against a well-known entertainment company. After days of heated back-and-forth discussion, the corporation agreed to return her money, but not before sliding a waiver under her nose that required that she never breathe a word about the incident. (She granted me an interview, then signed the nondisclosure statement and cashed the check. I held my story until the check cleared.)

Another favorite corporate strategy is taking legal action. A company either threatens to sue you or actually does. Such tactics never work with me, but customers fall for them regularly.

Scams are fueled by the misrepresentations or outright lies companies tell about themselves. As it turns out, some businesses can't help themselves since these fools actually delude themselves about their true purpose. Others try to mold your perception of them in order to persuade you to buy. Billions of dollars are at stake, and they know it.

Reputation management is the art of controlling key aspects of what people read about your company mostly online, but sometimes also in magazines, newspapers, and television. In the case of the Internet, their goal is to either delete all negative information from sites like Yelp or Google or Yahoo! or else push it to the bottom of any engine's results; and, of course, they try to bury bad reviews or beefs from disgruntled customers who paint them as unscrupulous or unresponsive.

Most corporations keep such reputation management triumphs to themselves. With good reason. If their customers knew or suspected that people they buy from were manipulating product information and recommendations, the tactic would backfire and tarnish their image rather than polish it.

But some can't shut up about their successes. Consider the predicament faced by Sensibill, a British telecommunications company, in 2010. A former employee had posted a negative review about the company online, and it was showing up high in the search-engine rankings. The company hired a reputation management company called Brag Interactive to not only "remove negative search engine listing(s)" from Google and other major search engines but also to increase search engine and organic traffic. That would bring in even *more* business by making its name show up higher in searches (more in Chapter 2, "I SEO You"). Brag Interactive implemented a comprehensive reputation management strategy that included building a new site for Sensibill. It taught employees how to manage their reputation themselves. "Our strategy proved to be a great success," Brag brags. "At one point the negative listing was deep in the search engine results."

Search-engine marketing firm Defend Matrix—one of the most established companies in this emerging and highly lucrative sector—makes incredibly bold promises to companies desperate to control their online reputations. Defend will "expand and solidify your online 'brand,'" according to its promotional material. Here is what's offered:

- Identifying "positive" web pages, blogs, forums, articles, or pages that it controls, that can be quickly elevated in the search engine rankings using optimization strategies. These pages then blanket and replace negative listings.
- Posting hundreds of positive articles (blog, journal, and forum entries), news items, press releases, and other pages on a steady basis.

These postings offer positive reflections on clients' reputations—but more importantly, they replace negative postings by taking the top positions on the sites in which they appear.

■ Creating new, positive content on your site and on sites that Defend Matrix controls, and then optimizing this content so that it rises quickly to the top search-engine rankings. Defend Matrix owns hundreds of sites for this purpose.

The result? Consumers are far less likely to find reviews from disgruntled customers who would warn you about a bad company and *more* likely to see contrived glowing write-ups from adoring clients.

What Do Companies Think of Themselves?

If you've ever wondered how modern-day companies see themselves, click over to the Footnoted blog (www.footnoted.com), created by Michelle Leder, author of the 2003 book *Financial Fine Print: Uncovering a Company's True Value*. Footnoted digs deep into company earnings reports and SEC filings to unearth the exaggerations and misrepresentations companies tell themselves—and investors.

■ Even as pharmacy retail chain Rite-Aid congratulated itself for its excellent service initiatives in regulatory filings, it was unable to stock some of the basic necessities in its stores, much to the disappointment of its customers.

■ Managers of now-defunct Northwest Airlines and Continental Airlines lavished generous compensation on departing executives while their companies' customer-service rankings circled the drain. The message? "Good job, fellas." (Or maybe, "Screw you, customers!")

■ Despite the fact that one Las Vegas resort announced "aggressive" cutbacks during the last recession that almost certainly affected its customer service, it signed an exceptionally generous contract with a longtime executive, raising

(continued)

(*continued*)

    his pay by more than 50 percent. I guess everyone took a hit during an economic downturn except the senior executives.

    If you think these sound like the words and actions of delusional companies that have lost touch with not only their own customers but with the very idea of customer service—take a bow. These examples suggest that companies have nowhere near a grasp on reality.

Avoiding Sock Puppets

The lengths companies go to shape an opinion can be mind-boggling. For example, in 2007 Whole Foods CEO John Mackey was outed as the guy behind the online ID "Rahodeb." He'd reportedly used the Yahoo! account anonymously to badmouth rival chain Wild Oats right before his company acquired it. After Mackey's clumsy efforts were discovered, the deal was put in jeopardy. This strain of reputation management, in which a company's employee assumes an alter ego, is called *sock puppeting*. It has evolved in ways most consumers would find very troubling. In 2011, it was revealed that the U.S. military is developing an application that secretly manipulates social media sites by faking online personas to influence online conversations. That's sock puppetry on a massive scale.

We're just at the beginning of the rep management revolution, if it can be called that. A 2010 survey by executive recruiters Korn/Ferry International found that 59 percent of executives believe the recent increase in awareness of corporate reputation risk will affect a board's view of reputation management and crisis preparedness. Only 28 percent said the shift has no effect, while 13 percent were unsure of how the focus on corporate reputation would impact the company. That's a lot of room for growth.

The takeaway? Be skeptical. *Very* skeptical. "Remember, not everything written on the Internet is true," says Abraham Shafi, co-founder of social media site Veechi Corp. Shafi's advice is particularly important in the Information Age, where anything published online is accepted as fact.

Since the early days of social media there have been stories of "rep-management" mills–organizations in third-world countries where underpaid workers populate forums, websites, and discussion groups with flattering material about a company. The evidence of their work is everywhere—yet in a sense it's nowhere. Can anyone prove these "cockroaches'" existences? If so, where is the smoking gun?

Consider the case of Billy, a former restaurateur in Costa Rica. He contacted me in 2010 to confess that as a one-man rep-management mill he'd brought his competitors' reputations down a notch or two. His weapon of choice: popular travel ratings site TripAdvisor (www.tripadvisor.com). ·

He explained:

I began tracking feedback about my restaurant on TripAdvisor's "rants and raves" page. It very quickly occurred to me that I could write in glowing reviews about my own restaurant and up my ratings numbers.

After a period of time, I began to see my ratings slide a bit after some not so [complimentary] postings by supposedly "real" customers. The complaints that were [cited] seemed somewhat contrived; and as owner and general manager I would have become aware very quickly about these types of complaints [had they been genuine].

Were [these comments] posted by my competition? Perhaps. So I simply got on TripAdvisor and bombarded them with glowing reviews about my own restaurant. Within days, I was rated a perfect 5!

Does this sound too good to be true? Well, it's frequently how things are done. So, in order to make more people aware of these kinds of practices I happily connected Billy with a producer from the *Today* show where he appeared on a segment about reputation management on February 17, 2011.

Marketing experts who spoke to me actually consider Billy an amateur. Now imagine his casual efforts to influence his restaurant's reputation magnified exponentially by an army of thousands of underpaid content-mill workers, each of whom has dozens of aliases with which to seed discussion boards and forums with favorable—or unfavorable—comments.

Worse, consumers can't tell if a company's reputation is managed. If it's done correctly, no one should be the wiser. In fact, according to Gary Bahadur, former Bank of America senior vice president and author of *Privacy Defended: Protecting Yourself Online*, "The only way [to tell] would be to see how quickly they respond to a negative attack." A fine example of a managed reputation is web-hosting company Network Solutions, which reacted to a security breach with lightning speed. "Their reputation management team was out responding to blogs and putting out news stories the same day," Bahadur says, "all [of which were] very positive responses." This upbeat feedback overwhelmed any negative comments and pushed them to the bottom of the search results or marginalized them, turning the break-in into a non-event.

How to Find Better Service

As a general rule, a company with an active reputation management program will be concerned—almost to the point of being paranoid— about any potentially negative review posted online. I have spoken with many savvy customers who, when disappointed with a product or service, promised to share their displeasure online and were promptly given what they asked for. (You'll find more on shaming companies in Chapter 14, "Turning a *No* Into a *Yes*.")

How Companies Manipulate Customers

But what's so terrible about a company trying to put its best foot forward? Nothing—and everything.

On the one hand, what company *wouldn't* want to enhance its status and squelch any negative publicity, particularly online, where information is thought to be freely exchanged, and where controlling a corporate message can be a challenge? On the other hand, there's no denying that these efforts are distorting reality and preventing prospective customers from getting an accurate picture of their company.

You deserve to know the whole truth about a business. What do past clients *really* think of the services they offer? How do they handle complaints? Are they worth patronizing? When you look for information, that's what you expect to find.

Of course, companies want you to think you've done your research and arrived at the conclusion that you should buy from them. In reality, those corporate executives engaged in this massive spin operation know for sure that their product or service isn't perfect. They're also aware that with some hard work and excellent reputation management, any company can drown out the cries of critics, bloggers, and consumer advocates who stand between them and your plastic.

And there lies the problem. Truth has become relative. To many businesses, you are nothing more than prey to be played with, manipulated, and devoured.

Executives know that people are more likely to give them their business if they believe the service is better. In a survey conducted by Harris Interactive, an overwhelming majority of respondents—85 percent—said they would be willing to pay more than the standard price of a good or service to ensure a superior customer experience. More than half said they'd be willing to pay 10 percent or more, and a noteworthy 1 in 10 said they'd pay 25 percent or more. That's a powerful incentive to control what's being said about you—and maybe to lie. "There will always be those who try to manipulate the system to their benefit," says Doug Wolfgram, chief executive of IntelliProtect, an online privacy service. "But they will be weeded out when good, solid products and services have good, solid online reputations." Let's drag out the old chestnut: You can't fool all the people all the time.

Selling Good Vibes on eBay, One Leaf at a Time

Here's an actual advertisement that appeared on Internet giant eBay, an online-only store where reputations are carefully cultivated and guarded by small and large businesses.

> Hello, for sale is a picture of a tree. This tree is an original and was taken by me. I have gotten nothing but 100% feedback from people from this picture. Great Picture! Once payment is made I will send you picture via email. Once payment is made and I send picture through email 100% feedback will be given to the buyer!!!! Once you pay for the
>
> *(continued)*

(*continued*)

item send me [an] eBay message with your email and I will email you the picture!

So if you pay 99 cents for a picture of this tree, I'll give you a 100 percent positive feedback rating. Clever, huh?

How We Fall for It

Is it any wonder that we make wrongheaded purchasing decisions when businesses from multinational corporations to the corner store are manipulating the facts about themselves? The conventional wisdom that positive reviews prime the cash pump has been unquestioned for decades. After all, our impression of a company directly affects what we buy, and that's particularly true of what's being said online. If we see a glowing write-up, we're more likely to buy something.

A 2005 study by the London School of Economics found (not surprisingly) that reputations and sales go hand in hand. A positive rep translates to higher sales, while a negative reputation drags it down to headshaking levels. Other research has more closely tied that to online activity, which is where most rep management takes place nowadays.

Retailers know that online reputations are important, and they are becoming even more aware of this truth. As such, they are shifting more resources into influencing the online conversation.

More Confessions of a Rep Manager

Sharon Geltner handles the management of reputations for a long list of corporate clients. Yet she admits that some of her would-be customers deserve a worse rap. As she explained, "I've gotten pleas from an apartment complex owner and a lawyer who were losing tenants and clients, respectively, because of their bad online reputations. The lawyer had to get out of his practice and turned to self-publishing as a way to buttress his rep and ego. The sad part is, they deserved their reputations, and simply weren't willing to clean up their acts in real life." She's quick to add that she turned both clients down.

Sometimes even reputation management can't save a company from itself.

Think about how you shop. When you see a product with a constellation of star ratings do you feel better about buying it? *I* do. A 2007 Berkeley study suggests we rely on customer ratings, particularly when we shop online, to assure ourselves that the product we see "is reflective of the product that will be shipped" and that the sellers are not deceitful or negligent. Customers are "very sensitive" to ratings, and easily swayed by them.

It is far more difficult to say how much consumers spend because of the ratings. I've sat across from executives who claim that half a star can mean millions of dollars of business in a single year, but even they really can't prove this (and if they could, would they *ever* open the books up to a consumer advocate?). I will not be going out on a limb by estimating that between one-third and one-half of all consumer purchases are influenced by consumer reviews. However, whether that influence was actually responsible for one-third to one-half of all consumer purchases is an unanswered question.

Transparent Lies

The next time a company claims to be transparent, take note— because although the term *transparency* is often corporate-speak for openness and honesty, transparency is a measure of what a company *does*, not what it *says*. When a company claims to be transparent, this often means it's hiding something, the reverse of the word's definition. The best example of this is the airline industry, which has claimed to be completely transparent while

(continued)

(*continued*)

hiding billions of dollars in fees from its passengers—fees imposed only *after* customers have agreed to buy a ticket. But banks and wireless companies enact similar transparency in charging frustrated clients.

I watched these transparency dramas from afar until I became ensnared in one of my own: A client who repeatedly claimed to be transparent while at the same time spinning an impressive web of lies. I say "impressive" because it wasn't a global conglomerate but a small media company with only a few employees.

But the lesson wasn't lost on me. Now, when someone claims to be transparent, an alarm goes off. I've come to the conclusion that real transparency isn't a corporate slogan; it's part of a company's DNA.

"SocialSpark Loves Your Blog"

Since 1997, I've run a website (www.elliott.org) that gets decent traffic numbers; so I receive a fair number of unsolicited offers. It takes a few seconds on the site to figure out that my primary goal is to advocate for consumers. So I was surprised when I received an e-mail from a key player in the rep management racket called Izea.

"I'm reaching out to you to discuss a possible partnership with your blog," the form letter started. "I came across your site and after looking around your blog, I thought it might be a great fit for our site!"

Clearly, they didn't spend *any* time there. If they had, they'd know I'd be dead set against signing up for a service like theirs. Why? Izea works as a middleman between big companies who want to increase their social media exposure and bloggers who are hungry for a quick buck made through PayPal. It's pay for play; I write about one of these companies on my site, make it look like an authentic post, and I get paid anywhere from $200 to $500 per post. And the companies participating in these campaigns are not bottom-feeders. They include brand names like Microsoft, HP, LG, and Virgin. While Izea claims to offer clear disclosure of the sponsored nature of these posts, most readers probably don't pay attention to the fine print. The campaign looks like an authentic word-of-mouth recommendation.

Don't Fall for a Managed Reputation

Companies covet a sterling reputation even when they don't have one. They want to be the next Amazon.com, Kohl's, or Costco (the top-rated companies in a 2011 customer ranking by the Temkin Group). Some companies see rep management (RM) as a shortcut. Here's how to spot them.

- *Read the negative customer reviews in context.* Does the company respond to the review and address the problem, or just ignore it? Disregarding a review may indicate that the company just wants to whitewash its reputation.
- *Look for patterns.* Are there a lot of positive or negative reviews? Does every product get five stars, or one star? If so, then there's a good likelihood the process is rigged by the company's employees or a consultant.
- *Be on the lookout for one-time posters with the "-est" syndrome.* Someone who posts only one glowingly positive (or terribly negative) rating is the corporate plant; for example: "This was the *best* movie ever" or "This is the *nicest* car on the market." If the central message being conveyed is *this is the best product or service ever—run.* Chances are, you're reading the product of a managed reputation.

Businesses have badmouthed one another since the beginning of time. What's different today is that the stakes are higher and the methods more clever. If half a star can affect millions of dollars of business, how much money do you think a company will be willing to spend to influence the process? And putting words in *your* mouth and the mouths of thousands of customers—gee, how clever is *that*?

Companies are throwing untold resources into RM and the net result is that you can't trust anything you see online anymore. Anything. Those "customer" ratings? They're always rigged in one way or another. The Internet search engine results? Manipulated. Even comments on blogs and discussion groups are suspect at best.

Collectively, consumers are spending billions of dollars on products they wouldn't otherwise purchase—cars, electronics, and homes—of inferior value. The scams that lie behind this unfortunate trend can't be measured, but that doesn't make any of them any less a scam. But reputation management isn't the only way in which companies control what you see. The trickery extends to how we find information.

Rep Management Campaigns That Failed

Good reputation management happens quietly behind the scenes. Bad reputation management, however, can often be seen very clearly—and it's quite a spectacle. Take a front row seat:

- BP's handling of the *Deepwater Horizon* oil spill in 2010 is a classic case of reputation management gone wrong. Among its efforts: Buying oil-spill–related AdWords on Google after the disaster—which, unsurprisingly, didn't work. By then, BP's name had already become a punch line, and it will be forever synonymous with a disastrous gusher, connected like Exxon and *Valdez*.

- In 2008, the Canadian country music band *Sons of Maxwell* flew to Nebraska on United Airlines—and watched in horror as the airline's baggage handlers threw their expensive guitars into the cargo hold. Needless to say, the instruments were damaged beyond repair. United dragged its feet in fixing them, so the group turned the experience into a song and a heck of a humorous "viral" video entitled *United Breaks Guitars*. United launched a charm offensive, but only after the screw-up reportedly cost it $185 million. (In a way, United had given *Sons of Maxwell* a big break and exposure it had never dreamed of.)

- In 2011, a video of GoDaddy CEO Bob Parsons shooting an elephant in Zimbabwe made the rounds. You'd think someone as Internet-savvy as Parsons would try to avert the damage with a sophisticated rep campaign. Instead he suggested that his critics were clueless, even after calls for a boycott against the domain name registration company. Of course, it's not always so horrible for these doofuses. Months later, Bob sold his company for billions—but only after the uproar weakened GoDaddy's brand.
- In 2011, Legacy Learning Systems was charged with seeding the Internet with fake product reviews for expensive DVD guitar courses. According to the FTC, the endorsements generated more than $5 million in sales of Legacy's courses. Legacy settled the claim for $250,000, which for them was the cost of doing business.

2

I SEO You

Never send a human to do a machine's job.

—Agent Smith, *The Matrix*

"WE'RE BEING BLACKMAILED," my friend Scott said, his voice cracking on the phone. I half expected him to confess they'd found an X-rated tape with him in a starring role. Instead, he e-mailed me a web address.

"What am I looking at here?" I asked Scott, a former colleague I'd stayed in touch with after our Internet venture folded in the 1990s. He explained that someone—he wasn't entirely sure who—had posted a negative review of his company, which specialized in acquiring patents, to two of the most popular gripe sites. "The content of the complaints is wildly off base," he said. "It describes services we don't even offer." Worse, the grievances had suddenly and mysteriously risen to the top of Google's rankings. So when anyone typed in his company's name, the complaint showed up first. The unscrupulous gripe site, far from being cooperative, agreed to remove the complaint—for a fee. This didn't make sense to Scott. Why pay to have something removed that wasn't even true?

17

That was my first exposure to the underside of search engine optimization (SEO). Think about how you browse the Net, and you know you're being watched. You probably wouldn't consider making a major purchase until you've Googled it. As I said in the last chapter, search engine results are often rigged by companies who use excruciatingly followed-through reputation management (RM). But sometimes, companies also use devious SEO strategies to shape the results from behind the scenes.

In Scott's case, a shady website was using that technique to shake down his business. The gripe site had built a network of sites that simply referred back to its page, ensuring a high search-engine ranking and top placement for all of its content. Too smart to be legal or moral. But it's more commonly deployed by companies to dupe their customers.

SEO isn't bad, but in the wrong hands it can drive tens of thousands of customers to make uninformed decisions, from buying a pair of glasses from a disreputable merchant to purchasing school supplies from an underhanded e-tailer. Like reputation management, companies tend to view these acts as victimless crimes. Yet they are not.

Try a search for a competitive term like "Viagra" or "weight loss" to see how SEO works. Some of the results deliver meaningful information and clearly belong there, but a huge number of links take you to storefronts selling illegal pharmaceuticals or obvious sham diets. Almost without exception, someone used search engine optimization to propel those pitches and ads to the top.

Scott's company eventually rid itself of the negative review, but not through conventional means. Google caught on to the site's SEO sins and lowered its page rankings (Google's results are called "pages" after founder Larry Page), relegating the review to its rightful place at the bottom.

Consumers aren't so lucky—usually. Almost every major company uses SEO to improve its online standings. It really has no choice. The higher the ranking, the more clicks. How much is the top spot on Google worth? According to a 2010 survey by Optify, being number one drove 34 percent of *all* traffic, almost as much as the numbers 2 through 5 slots combined. Anything beyond the first screen is pretty much ignored.

What's less clear is the effect that wholesale manipulation of search engines is having on your buying experience. Companies shrug it off, saying their SEO initiatives are merely out there to get its sites seen. But as a customer, your instincts are already telling you this "corporate tool" called SEO could easily get you scammed.

How to Save Money

SEO has already cost you money because you've almost certainly made a purchase from a site that, in a sleazy way, artificially raised its ranking. By clicking on multiple search engines and reading past the first page of results, you're less likely to get fooled the next time. In addition to Google, try Bing (www.bing.com), Yahoo! (www.yahoo.com), and Dogpile (www.dogpile.com), which combines many search results in a single return. Remember that the best SEO can't fool all the search engines all the time.

A Scam That Wears Many Hats

SEO comes in three varieties:

1. *White-hat SEO* is a sensible and ethical way to make a page more search-engine friendly, like having a section for frequently asked questions or an "about" page and using the right keywords.
2. *Gray-hat SEO* is a little shadier and can involve paying someone to link to your site for purposes of boosting your content.
3. *Black-hat SEO* involves practices that are immoral, and in most states illegal, like hacking into another site and inserting a link, or spamming a site with comments intended to build links back to your site to raise your ranking. (Most of this work is done by companies who work in countries like Estonia and India.)

What Color Is Your SEO Hat?

In an anonymous survey of business managers, a majority claimed to be on the right side of the rules.

White	54 percent
Gray	31 percent
Black	15 percent

Source: CBS Interactive.

One company, TrendMetrix Software, described how it helped a Vancouver florist rise from obscurity to the #4 position on Google. It boasted of similar results for a lawyer's site: "Achieving a #1 ranking in this competitive local niche proves that with the right on and off page optimization strategy, our team can take any site to the top of Google," it promised. See? Why wouldn't a company make its sites more search-engine friendly?

Practically all companies claim to do white-hat SEO. But in my conversations with self-appointed SEO insiders, it became obvious that few understand the distinctions between white and gray or gray and black, or at least they pretended not to. Search engines continuously change the way they index and display sites, and SEO professionals like to cite the shifting ground as reasons why these rules should remain fluid. But that gives companies more wiggle room than they deserve.

Most SEO professionals keep a low profile, but sometimes they'll tell you what they did. And if you're really lucky, they will inform on how they did it.

The SEO Pitch

You can learn quite a bit by the way an SEO company pitches itself to a prospective client. Here's an actual form letter I received, which I've annotated with my comments.

We are leading SEO service provider and web Development Company. We are expert in PHP,.NET, and many open sources like Joomla, Drupal, Wordpress, Oscommerse, Zencart and Blog Management.

[We're throwing a lot of acronyms and hot terms around to impress you. But the fact is we can't even spell. Also, if you're smart enough to build your site on a free content management system and follow some basic design principles, you don't need us.]

We offer best of quality work to our clients at the lowest possible prices. We can quickly promote your website.

[We're desperate, perhaps because we haven't mastered the English language.]

We can place your website on top of the Natural Listings on Google, Yahoo!, and MSN.

[We are making the patently impossible claim that we can guarantee you a "top" ranking and the ridiculous assumption that you care about Yahoo! and MSN, or rather Bing, sorry for the error, in the hope you are really, really dumb.]

We do not use "link farms" or "black hat" methods that Google and the other search engines frown upon and can use to de-list or ban your site.

[We're black-hatters all the way, dude.]

Price is never a constraint with us because we take pride in handling challenging work.

[We're *really* hard up.]

We would be happy to send you best fit proposal for web development and designing and if you have a SEO requirement we will send you a proposal using the top search phrases for your area of expertise.

In order for us to respond to your request for information, please include your company's website address (mandatory) and/or phone number.

[We don't really know who you are. We're sending out this spam to a random list. Never mind that spamming you is a crime, too.]

Is Your Site Rigged?

Grey- and black-hat SEO practitioners don't exactly hang out a shingle in front of their electronic store. But you can spot them if you look for these red flags:

- Do they use *hidden text* or *hidden links*? If you select a portion of the page, this "hidden" content will often be visible.
- Do you click on one link expecting to go to one page but find yourself on another page instead? That's called a "sneaky redirect," and it's used to fool search engines and users.
- Does the content not fit the search? Sometimes, unscrupulous (and well-trained) web designers will load a site up with irrelevant keywords that are meant to attract visitors who wouldn't otherwise come.
- Does the site try to persuade you to download something like a "free" application? Don't go there. It's probably trouble and can cause a virus to open on your computer.
- Does the site have little original content or just try to get you to click on an affiliate link? Those can also be hallmarks of a black-hatter.

SEO Gone Wild

How can Google's trusted and super secret algorithm, the very thing that lets you find almost anything on the number-one search engine, be gamed? It's not really that hard.

JCPenney managed to rise to the top of Mount Google for practically everything it sold on its site, JCPenney.com, by placing links back to it on hundreds of seemingly unrelated sites. Some of the sites only contained links—a clear attempt to illegally gain favor with search engines, who reward sites with higher placement when more sites link back to them. After an investigation the retailer fired its SEO firm.

Online retailer Overstock.com took a slightly different but no less questionable approach to winning the search engine game by offering a 10 percent discount to university and college-affiliated sites that linked to it. Educational websites with a .edu in their address rather than .com are more highly valued by Google.

Or how about the contrarian strategy used by a tiny New York–based online eyeglasses retailer DecorMyEyes.com? It actually tried to garner negative customer reviews online by taking advantage of a Google flaw (now fixed) that failed to distinguish between positive and negative reviews. And it managed to do so surprisingly well, pushing its results to the top of the search results for designer glasses. Internet users mindlessly clicked on the links, even though they were up high for all the wrong reasons.

Google has now tweaked its search methodology to punish the retailers engaged in these black-hat SEO practices by lowering their rankings.

The smarty-pants unscrupulous SEO wizards, however, are never detected, and their work rewards their clients with top billing online and hundreds of millions in business they should not get. Chances are, you've been a victim and don't even know it.

How to Find Better Service

Nothing strikes fear in the heart of a manager like an angry customer with a respectable Klout score. Klout (www.klout.com), of course, measures your social media mojo, and the more followers, blog readers, or "friends" you have online, the likelier a company is to provide top-notch service. If not, there's a very real chance that your discontent could neutralize months of expensive SEO efforts. Don't be afraid to let a company know—in the loudest voice possible—you have a PC, tablet computer, or smartphone, and aren't afraid to use it.

Imagine if the world was turned around, we lived in a fantasy land, and you could implicitly trust the results of an Internet search.

What if you knew you'd get to the right page every time, as opposed to the page that had the budget to hire a crooked SEO consultant? In that perfect world, how would your shopping patterns change? What bogus products or services would you *not* fall for?

Unfortunately, Internet search results—the very thing that drives commerce in the twenty-first century—are completely rigged. And *we* are the targets.

The lesson is this: don't automatically trust what you see when you conduct a search online, and don't rely on a single search engine. Most important, be skeptical of anything and everything you find. The former JCPenney.com's and Overstock.com's of the present day are *nothing* compared to what awaits us as the hatters get more sophisticated.

Reputation management and SEO aren't the only tools available to companies to spin lies about themselves. They also use more direct methods, such as disseminating misleading product claims.

Who's spinning the truth? There are helpful lists that identify the best and worst companies, but as I'll note in a moment, they aren't necessarily an indicator of company-wide rep management and SEO efforts. The University of Michigan's authoritative American Customer Service Index assigns industries and individual companies a grade of 1–100, based on customer feedback. This offers a quick and concise picture of how customers feel, for real. Another customer dissatisfaction gauge is the Customer Service Hall of Shame, compiled once a year by the polling firm Zogby International for MSN.

The latest poll found the following 10 companies had most complaints about service:

1. Bank of America
2. AOL
3. Capital One
4. Sprint
5. Time-Warner
6. Comcast
7. Citigroup
8. Progressive
9. JPMorgan Chase
10. Farmers Insurance

You might assume that the executives at these companies are locked in meetings busily allocating the largest possible budget to up their propaganda efforts. Not necessarily. Have a look at the flip side—the Hall of Fame:

1. Amazon.com
2. Trader Joe's
3. Netflix
4. Nordstrom
5. Publix Supermarkets
6. Southwest Airlines
7. Apple
8. Federal Express
9. Costco Warehouse
10. United Parcel Service

Notice anything about *this* list? The companies with the greatest customer service reputation also are known to control corporate messaging, from secretive Trader Joe's and Apple to social-media–savvy Southwest Air. You can't help but wonder if the customers who gave Amazon.com, Trader Joe's, and Netflix high marks for customer service weren't really rewarding them for the fabulous shape of their corporate messages.

Maybe managers at AOL, Bank of America, and Comcast just don't see the point of controlling what people read or hear about them; or perhaps they don't understand it as well as their competitors. Could it be that, like their inferior customer-service programs, they simply don't care what people think? Either way it would be a mistake to assume that these are the best, or worst, of corporate America. Rather, it would be fair to assume they are the best and worst at *managing their images* through SEO and reputation management.

Above the Law?

Is all of this massaging of the facts legal? The answer is perhaps the most troubling aspect of these unsettling marketing trends: Absolutely. Companies that indulge in these practices break no rules.

If anything, an argument can be made that our government assists in these efforts to *keep* information from consumers.

Try to find the answer to this seemingly simple question: How many airline passengers complain about bad service? The major U.S. airlines are under no obligation to tell, so they don't. The federal government counts only grievances that passengers file with its Aviation Enforcement Division, which is a small fraction of the total, and even these are aggregated and disclosed monthly in a way that is nearly impossible to decipher.

The picture gets even more dismal when it comes to general consumer complaints. The Federal Trade Commission, our leading and most official consumer-protection agency, does not require companies to report complaints by customers in any systematic way. Though the agency collects a bit of complaint data, it does so by category, not company—which is profoundly unhelpful for someone trying to make an informed buying decision.

So reputation management is not just legal; it's getting a hand from the U.S. government. But things are not hopeless. Look behind the scenes at any business, large or small, and you'll see many forces at work. It would be inaccurate to think of corporate America as a monolith that always acts with one purpose even though it sometimes seems that way. Companies face competition and a changing industry landscape every day, and, same as it always is, they rely on customers like you to remain highly profitable.

This is exactly why the war on information can only be won by the consumer. Because despite efforts to control everything you see and hear about them, and despite their wild successes, companies don't control the way you spend your money. *You*, the consumer, do.

Historically, the most reliable way to wrest your hard-earned dollars out of your purse is through the power of words. But it doesn't have to be that way.

3

Fooled You

Man's mind is so formed that it is far more susceptible to falsehood than to truth.

—Desiderius Erasmus

ON ITS WEBSITE, the bed-and-breakfast on Maryland's Eastern Shore looked ideal for a quiet country weekend. A wide-angle shot of its English garden and immaculate parlor displaying antique furniture and artwork, not to mention the proprietor's invitation to experience the small inn's "unique" hospitality, were all I needed to convince me to secure a nonrefundable reservation with my credit card.

When my girlfriend and I arrived in town to check in on that summer day in 1997, I parked just short of the property and soon realized that the neighborhood was iffy at best. Dilapidated cars, some apparently abandoned, cluttered the street. The English garden was overgrown with weeds. The property looked like the old *Addams Family* mansion—before it was renovated for the TV show.

We'd been duped.

Merchants have been lying about their products and services since the dawn of humankind, of course. But the latest technology, able to track the limits of consumer ignorance or indifference by the minute, has turned fibbing into an institutional art practiced by vendors from tiny hospitality companies to globe-straddling conglomerates.

The lies hit us hardest when we most want to believe them. Take green products. Who doesn't want to help save the environment? However, one survey found that 98 percent of products that claimed to be green were no such thing. Consider the results shown in Figure 3.1.

It's clear that many companies find it perfectly acceptable to stretch the truth in order to encourage a sale. And these misstatements can range from little white lies like "Satisfaction Guaranteed or Your Money Back" to outright fraud. Sophisticated consumers are aware that companies have a different concept of the truth, which is to say it's all relative when the corporation is trying to make its numbers. But do they know how far a business is willing to go to bilk you?

The bed-and-breakfast that awaited us certainly exaggerated more than a few facts to snare our business in a pre–TripAdvisor era, and I was stopped in my tracks. I felt completely powerless, because I hadn't yet embarked on a career as a consumer advocate. I phoned the proprietor and informed him I wouldn't be able to make it. He demanded I pay for the entire weekend, but I said if he billed my credit card I would dispute the charges. After a brief but spirited argument, we finally compromised and I paid for one night. Another lesson learned.

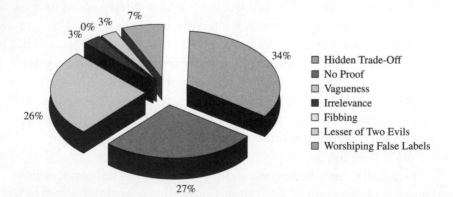

Figure 3.1 How Companies Mislead Consumers

Denominator = total sins committed.

But *Everyone's* Doing It

It's hard to find a company that isn't fudging the truth somehow. But only a fraction of these corporate misstatements get the attention of the Federal Trade Commission, the nation's top cop to corporate America. It's still worth considering some of the agency's recent enforcement actions:

- A $28 million fine in 2010 against Debt.com Marketing and two other companies for deceptively claiming they could save consumers thousands of dollars by reducing their credit card debt. Instead, the companies merely sold the sales leads generated by their ads to debt settlement providers or to other lead generators or lead brokers that resold them, according to the government.
- An $11.5 million fine in 2009 against Federal Loan Modification Law Center, which charged up to $3,000 for a "Federal Loan Modification program." But the modification wasn't all it was cracked up to be, says the government. Though the company charged consumers anywhere from $1,000 to $3,000 in fees for their services—much of which had to be paid up-front—it failed in numerous instances to obtain the promised loan modifications. The company also neglected to answer or return consumers' calls or provide updates about the status of their loan modifications and assured consumers that negotiations with their lenders were proceeding when, in fact, little or no effort had been made to contact the lenders.
- A $2.1 million fine in 2010 against NBTY, whose subsidiaries make children's multivitamins featuring characters such as the Disney Princesses, Winnie the Pooh, Nemo from *Finding Nemo*, and Spider-Man. The government alleged the manufacturer had made deceptive claims about the amount of an Omega-3 fatty acid called DHA contained in its vitamins, as well as unsupported claims that a daily serving of the products promotes healthy brain and eye development in children.

It's not always the money they lose that hurts the most. In 2010, investigators found Dannon guilty of exaggerating the health benefits of its Activia yogurt and DanActive dairy drink, two popular products shilled by actress Jamie Lee Curtis that contain beneficial bacteria known as probiotics. And even though Activia still makes similar claims today, the company agreed to pay $21 million for this deceit. The government also ordered the company to stop claiming that Activia relieves temporary irregularity. In the end, the Feds said the company could continue to make its claims only if the representation was "non-misleading and the ad conveys that eating three servings a day is required to obtain the benefit," or unless Dannon had additional scientific proof of its claims. Getting caught is also a cost of doing business. And the above cases represent just a fraction of the scams that truth-impaired companies perpetrate on consumers. To get a more accurate picture, talk to the FBI, which estimates so-called white-collar crimes cost Americans between $300 and $660 billion annually. According to the 2010 National Public Survey on White Collar Crime, chances are good that you or someone in your immediate family is a victim of a shady business. Nearly one in four households has experienced at least one form of white-collar crime. The most common business-to-consumer crimes? Price misrepresentation and unnecessary repairs. And get this—just 11 percent of the victims reported these crimes to law enforcement, preferring to contact their bank or credit card to retrieve their money.

We're probably *all* victims of misleading, and maybe fraudulent, offers as consumers with money. A lot of scammers get away with their crimes because these deeds go unreported to law enforcement. Only the most flagrant offenders ever get brought to justice.

Most businesses don't regard service as yet another line item on their balance sheets. They see anyone who expects them to stand behind the products as a liability. And they won't think twice about telling a tall tale. To them, we're often nothing more than a dollar sign—a means to an end. Have a look at the results of this anonymous survey of business managers.

Have You Ever Lied to a Customer?

Yes	47 percent
No	53 percent

Source: CBS Interactive.

How to Save Money

Most of the scams I've described so far are what are normally called lowercase scams, which means they're obviously shady and are fairly easy to discover. Reading this will sharpen your senses and arm you with the tools to spot them. But what many customers don't realize is that when a big corporation is caught doing something wrong and signs a settlement agreement, you are likely due compensation—even for something as small as a surprise fee. Unfortunately, many consumers fail to pay much attention to the settlement notices, which look like junk mail or worse, and they miss a valuable opportunity for payback. And revenge is best served as a check.

When it comes to misleading customers, let's just say it's a team effort. More than one in three senior managers and company directors in a survey claim it's acceptable for their employees to tell white lies to customers, and nearly half say it's okay to misstate facts if somehow it safeguards the firm. Three-quarters of workers polled by Microsoft feel they are forced to lie at work and about half admit to doing it. And consider these examples:

- Office supply retailer Office Depot has told customers who weren't willing to spend enough on optional product protection plans that the computers they wanted were not in stock—even if they were. The reason is that sales associates are under such intense pressure to sell extras that they'd rather tell a tall tale than make a bad sale.
- Cable provider Cablevision tried to convince subscribers to upgrade to digital cable boxes and digital service by claiming the FCC was mandating the switchover. Our Federal Communications Commission had never said any such thing. The ruse potentially netted the cable company millions of extra revenue—$6.50 a month for the new boxes and $10.95 for digital service.
- Even Apple, which has one of the most favorable reps for customer service, sometimes instructs its employees to bend facts. They reportedly tell consumers that unlocking their iPhone will

make them stop working and that switching to a rival service provider on a jailbroken phone will "fry the antenna"—neither of which is true. (Car companies say the same with aftermarket products the automaker isn't selling you.)

Customers can give just as good as they take. After all, we assume if companies lie to us, we should do the same back at them. We do—and the fibbing starts at an early age. Nearly two-thirds of American high school students admit to cheating on a test, said a comprehensive study by the Josephson Institute. An astounding 8 in 10 people confess to lying in job interviews, according to another poll. And nearly 6 in 10 Americans in a Kelton Research study say they've swiped products from their employer for personal use at home, known officially as pilfering (it's a sport!). Additionally:

- *Hotel guests* are in a class by themselves when it comes to dishonest behavior. The most common item swiped by travelers? The easy-to-pack washcloth. A survey by the online agency Travelocity found 86 percent of hotel guests admitted to taking toiletries like soap and gel, some of which hotels allow you to bring home. About 3 percent said they had swiped a bathrobe or slippers (you'll usually get charged for the former), and 1 percent confessed to stealing dishes, silverware, electronics, and Bibles. (Bibles? Whatever happened to "Thou shalt not steal"?) All told, hotel guests steal up to $100 million of goods a year, according to the American Hotel & Lodging Association. Some savvy hotel chains have started stores to sell whatever is in your room. Maybe the joke is on us.
- While reports of *customers lying to businesses* don't typically make headlines, incidents happen routinely. People bend the truth about prices to gain an advantage or to make them appear more qualified to make a purchase. That said, about 35 in every 10,000 mortgage applications are found to be fraudulent. In my experience the most common customer problem isn't the bald-face lie but omitting the important facts, such as the product being out of warranty or the product having been used in a way that voids the warranty.

- Even behavior like the ones above has the potential to destroy entire industries and has a ripple effect in the economy. Let's take a look at illegal file sharing, which is unthinkingly justified by many consumers. People claim that movies and albums are over-priced and these are victimless crimes, or that digital rights management (DRM) is too restrictive. Some will not even argue that it's a victimless crime; they simply declare that the victims deserve it. That's harsh.

Connect the dots, and it is clear that we must address the dysfunctional relationship between companies and consumers. And soon. No one wants to live in a scam-or-be-scammed world, where either they sell you a bill of goods or you do the same.

We simply can't go on like this.

Little White Lies

Consumer reporters are obsessed with headline-grabbing stories, like Bernard Madoff's $50 billion Ponzi scheme or the subprime loan scandal that almost destroyed the world economy. Those *are* blockbuster stories, and I can't blame the media for covering them *ad nauseam*. But many journalists are lazy, and they go after the lowest-hanging fruit because, yes, it's easier to cover than a small fraud that is disrupting everyday consumers' lives. These cads completely overlook the everyday damage caused by companies who misrepresent their products in a small way. Little white lies earn dishonest companies a few pennies here and there, but they all add up. And they can account for the bulk of the scams when you start doing a little math.

What are some little white lies? A colleague of mine at MSNBC .com, Bob Sullivan, presented a disturbing laundry list of such misrepresentations in his excellent 2007 book entitled *Gotcha Capitalism: How Hidden Fees Rip You Off Every Day—And What You Can Do About It*. Here are some standouts:

- *False labels*. Descriptions like "low fat" or "all natural" are probably the top offenders here. But what exactly *do* these phrases mean? For example, fast-food chain Wendy's introduced something called Natural Cut Fries in 2010. They looked natural, but apparently the only thing about them that was natural was that they were once potatoes. Turns out they're sprayed with sodium acid pyrophosphate and dusted with dextrose, a corn-based sugar. The fries also contain a silicone-based antifoaming agent, dimethylpolysiloxane. There's really nothing very natural-sounding about that. Same for the Duraflame Log, which claims its completely artificial fire starter today has "all new natural ingredients." Which in fact means nothing.

■ *Hidden fees*. Surprise fees or surcharges can appear anywhere from the Department of Motor Vehicles, which broadsides you with a convenience fee for paying by credit card—to the always-problematic telephone bill. Since Aleck Bell made that first call last century, the phone bill has always had questionable added charges; sometimes it seems like a game. Without wincing, take a look at your latest phone bill. How many extra fees are on there about which you have no idea why or when they began? Banks and credit cards are dreadful too, but perhaps none are worse than airlines. When hit by high fuel prices in 2008, these industries started engaging in a deceptive practice called unbundling—in other words, they systematically removed everything from the base price of a ticket and then charged customers separately for the various, uh, features. Air travelers thought they got the low fares they booked, until they showed up at the airport and learned that they had to pay extra for a seat assignment, to check a bag, to get a pillow, to be first in line for seats, to eat a snack on a transcontinental flight—the list is endless. The airlines have laughed all the way to the bank.

The airlines are overseen by the Federal Aviation Administration, a nearly-useless government org that was begun in the mid-twentieth century as a way to *promote* air travel.

■ *Price games*. Retailers deceive beloved customers with pricing practices that make their products look cheaper than they are. Padding is a retail practice of marking an item up and then discounting it to make it appear to be on sale when in fact it's likely still overpriced. You'll probably see this kind of white lie at the mall, although it can be done on a bigger scale and under the glare of the public spotlight. (All ads for Macy's actually state, "These sale items may have been offered at a lower price previously.") Oil companies were accused of padding their prices in 2005 after Hurricane Katrina, but they didn't bother discounting—they just padded and kept the difference. The Federal Trade Commission (FTC) investigated soaring energy prices and claimed to have found no widespread effort to manipulate the price of oil. This hardly came as a surprise, given that the Chairman and Commissioner of the FTC at the time was former ChevronTexaco lawyer Deborah Platt Majoras.

Businesses have an amazing ability to innovate when it comes to deception. When the government steps in to say that they can't charge a fee on one product, they invent another. For example, the Credit Card Accountability Responsibility and Disclosure Act enacted in 2009 made many credit card fees illegal. But by then clever credit card companies replaced a currency exchange fee with a foreign transaction fee and made more money with this new bone-headed charge and thanked the federal government for pushing them. Why? Under the old system a credit card company only charged an exorbitant exchange fee (often 2 percent of the value of a transaction) on a purchase made in a foreign currency. Under the new system, it applied fees to *any* purchase made with a foreign company—even if it was in U.S. dollars. This capacity for adapting their business quickly to the changing market and regulations is, I feel, *deception innovation.*

How to Find Better Service

When you suspect a product isn't all it's cracked up to be, you may also find a company unwilling to admit its shortcomings—and definitely not its deceptiveness. Yet at a management level, the company knows it's pulling a fast one and it doesn't want to invite outside scrutiny. That's why a polite statement saying that if your grievance isn't addressed you will swiftly take the matter to a regulatory or law-enforcement agency often gets things moving in the right direction. (For more on resolving complaints in a nonthreatening, but way cool, way, turn to the Appendix for a list of regulatory agencies.)

Who's to Say What's Bogus?

Not everyone can agree on the definition of *deceptive*. I asked my readers to submit their stories of being duped by companies, and two of the winners illustrate my point. They suggest that even when customers, lawmakers, or regulators step in and claim something is misleading, a business can easily respond with a slick and completely plausible answer that would prevail in court, if not also in the court of public opinion.

The first is a product called Ancestor Bands, a series of bracelets available online that claims to help you connect to your dead relatives. I'm serious.

"We are all uniquely connected to our ancestors genetically," the site says. "The bands you see here will help you tap into the proper frequencies that your Ancestors transmit throughout the Cosmos. They are desperately trying to connect with you and impart their Newfound Universal knowledge of the Universe." The bands will increase your mental power, physical strength, and reverse the effects of aging—all at the low price of $19.99! "Act now and you can connect to your pets, too!" Kidding.

As a natural skeptic, my first inclination is to crack up at this scam or anyone who'd fall for it. Humorist Barry Goldsmith told me he'd bought one. "I communicated with dead ancestors all right," he told me. "The dead ancestors of the owner of the Ancestor Bands company—who were laughing all the way to St. Peter's bank." But I don't know how ridiculous of an idea this is. I mean, if you could decisively *disprove* these bands allow you communicate with your ancestors, you'd also debunk half the world's organized religions. Who am I to say the bands won't work for someone? The FTC might quibble with its claims to increase your mental power and physical strength. Rightfully so. Dead ancestors are above a consumer advocate's pay grade.

Nomination number two comes from a company called Smart-Mouth, which has been billed as a revolutionary mouthwash that guarantees 12 hours of fresh breath. "With SmartMouth Mouthwash, one rinse in the morning and you'll have all day fresh breath," its TV ads claim. "One rinse at night and you can wake up with fresh breath. No more morning breath!" Bogus? That was my first thought. But the company sent me a product sample and asked me to try it. Unlike Ancestor Bands, there's some science behind SmartMouth. It uses a patented zinc-ion technology that supposedly freshens your breath and prevents new bad breath from forming.

The national advertising division of the Better Business Bureau (which tracks awful company claims brought to its attention by pro-active consumers) found SmartMouth provided a "reasonable basis" for its claims. And while I agree that the product works differently from other mouthwashes, and that it lasts longer, I would not recommend that anyone rely on a mouthwash for 12 hours of fresh breath. I base that on my own experience using SmartMouth. Nothing—and I really mean *nothing*—can overpower overspicy Italian food rich in garlic, pepper, and onions. It's the ultimate antimouthwash.

Point is, you can find a true believer who says his watch helps him talk with his dead grandfather, just as you can find a true skeptic who thinks the newest mouthwash is no better than Listerine. It's all a matter of perspective. But where is the limit? Where should the government step in and say, "That is complete crap!" It's hard to say. But mind the gap.

Businesses are not just aware of that gap; they exploit it. They create promotional messages that are heavy on hyperbole but light on detail, and so escape the scrutiny of regulators. These wrong product claims are misleading to most people but are technically legal. Is the government sanctioning these lies? To a lot of customers, and to me, they definitely are.

At least you know you're looking at an ad or a product claim and can ask these questions. But what if you didn't know where the message was coming from?

4

That's Not an Ad

Whatever deceives men seems to produce a magical enchantment.
—Plato

SOCIAL NETWORKING SERVICES like Foursquare let you check in from your mobile device and comment on places you've been, offering other friends tips on what to do—and not to do—when you're out and about. But *your* buddies aren't the only ones lurking on Foursquare and other location-based services such as Twitter and Facebook.

One "friend" of mine recently endorsed a popular hotel restaurant, but her picture gave her away: She was the property's public-relations director. The average user wouldn't have known, and probably assumed that she was a guest. Another friend recommended a bar at an airport without disclosing that he worked for the city's Convention & Visitors Bureau. Not cool.

Then I received an invitation:

I am writing from MyLikes, an ex-Google social media/Twitter advertising company that connects influencers on the web to advertisers. I wanted to send you an invite to be a premium influencer on MyLikes.

This is an invite-only program that allows power Twitter users such as yourself to make money by creating Sponsored Likes/ads for advertisers you choose and post them to Twitter. You get to set a price per tweet and accept/reject advertiser offers and write your own Sponsored Likes/Tweets. The minimum payout is extremely low ($2) and you get paid weekly through PayPal.

We are also running a contest to win a[n] Apple iPad. Given your following, you should have a significant chance of winning it.

Paying for tweets? You're kidding. Yet MyLikes is hardly alone. There are scores of other companies that will compensate you for placing their ads on your trusted social media channels. (I didn't respond to MyLikes; it wasn't to my "liking." Kim Kardashian did, though, and gets paid upwards of $10,000 for her tweets through another company. Her followers have no idea.)

When Your "Friends" Scam You

Most of us don't think twice when someone tries to friend or follow us online. But this might be a scam. Not only do people with promotional motives try to follow potential customers in order to sway their purchasing decisions, but sometimes their motives can be far darker. Some fraudsters have set up multiple Facebook accounts in an effort to gain your trust. The scheme gives the account the appearance of being trusted because the person has one or two mutual acquaintances. But once you accept their friend request, they try to reset your password, gaining access to your account. If you have more than 100 Facebook friends (some of whom are friends of friends, or acquaintances), watch out. At least one of them could be up to no good.

Advertising used to be easy to spot. Ads in magazines and newspapers looked noticeably different from news articles, thereby creating an unmistakable divide between what was paid for and what was editorial or journalism. TV ads popped up predictably, every seven or so minutes as program or pee breaks. But you can't be so sure when you run into an ad on the Internet, and companies like that.

Is the tweet you just saw from a friend really an endorsement—or a paid-for ad? What about the text message with a coupon code you just got on your mobile? Was the viral video somebody sent to you shot by a kid in his basement or produced by a Madison Avenue firm to look as if it were shot in a basement? You can't even trust the props in a movie; when the villain lights up a cigarette or a hero opens a can of soda, you can bet someone paid the producers for the placement. And ads? They're everywhere, from the basket you lay your laptop in at airport security to the error page you arrive at on your computer.

While the ad industry may consider these new ways of reaching you with their message to be "innovations," they are in fact far more than that. Old-school advertising was engaging and even entertaining—we still remember the jingles of yore. But it never pretended to be more than a message paid for by a company. Today's advertising boldly steps outside those lines, becoming a part of the stories you see and the word-of-mouth recommendations you hear.

Much of today's commercial advertising is equal parts promotion and misrepresentation.

Corporate America spends $125 billion a year on traditional ads that include radio, TV, and print. It shells out another $24 billion for online ads. But what is an online ad? Buying an AdWord on Google or a banner on Yahoo! comes to mind, and maybe purchasing a text ad on a popular newsletter or blog. But you have to think *bigger*. "Online" can mean anything from paying bloggers to write glowing reviews of your products to sponsoring a tweet. The most sinister (and often most effective) forms of online advertising don't look like ads, but instead are what company insiders call organic mentions. While they appear to be authentic and impartial comments, these are sponsored and sophisticated corporate messages sent as though by a pal.

Product Placement in Songs

Everyone knows about product placements on TV or film, where advertisers pay a production company to integrate their merchandise in the script. Three super-famous examples are FedEx in the Tom Hanks film *Cast Away*, Reese's Pieces in

(continued)

(*continued*)

E.T., and the neverending use of Subway in the comedy *Happy Gilmore* and on NBC's struggling comedy *Chuck*. In some cases, particularly in the latter case, the brands are used as more than asides—they are central plot devices.

But did you know product placements aren't limited to TV and movies? For example, the Kluger Agency will place your product in a song for a fee that ranges between $75,000 to "over seven figures," according to founder Adam Kluger. He connects advertisers like Cadillac and Penthouse with A-listers such as Lady Gaga and T-Payne, helping them weave product mentions into their songs. A guy like Kluger also brokers deals between advertisers and artists to write music video treatments around the brands and products rather than trying to squeeze the products into an existing storyline. Check out Britney Spears' video for *Hold It Against Me*, and you'll see repeated references to the dating site PlentyOfFish .com—which paid through the nose ring for the mention. They've managed to achieve seamless integration, I guess.

Do customers know they're hearing or watching an ad? Kluger claims between 25 to 30 percent of audiences are aware they're watching a musical product placement. "It depends on what type of artist it is," he says. "Someone like Justin Bieber's audience isn't really aware yet. But a group like Lady Antebellum, with a more mature audience who are better versed in these types of things, would be more aware."

How They Lie

Whatever lies behind advertisers' shift from respecting the boundaries between product pitches and editorial content to camouflaging the former in the latter—whether the reason is technology, pressure from shareholders, or good old-fashioned avarice—here we are. No part of our lives seems off limits to corporate messaging. It's even tougher to measure the damage that this relentless spinning does to people who actually care about what they buy. It is one thing to know you're being assaulted by ads and another to *not* know you're being assaulted by ads. This much is certain: Online ad spending—online being the primary vehicle for delivering nontraditional ads—is soaring with no end in sight.

Online Ad Spending	
Year	Spending (in $millions)
2000	$8,087
2005	$12,542
2010	$25,727
2015	$41,417 (projection)

Source: Deutsche Bank.

Those are big numbers. And while it's difficult to say how much these campaigns influence you, here are some estimates. One measure is the expected return on investment in an ad campaign. No one continues to buy ads that do not drive business. So let's say that for every dollar spent on advertising a company gets three dollars' worth of business, which is conservative. Now triple the numbers shown in the chart. By 2015, businesses will spend $41 billion and they'll get at least $124 billion in business, some of that from you. And I'm willing to bet a good portion of it would have been spent elsewhere, were it not for that ad. It's all a matter of trust (see Figure 4.1).

Here are the three areas where companies are hitting you hardest with subterfuge:

1. *Mobile.* With close to 5 billion mobile phones worldwide, it's easy to see the appeal of advertising through your handset. What's more, many of these mobiles are smartphones, which means they can do tons more besides send and receive calls. Today, base models come equipped with GPS chips that pinpoint your location (made into FCC law last decade), thereby allowing you to participate in any number of location-based social networks. All of this adds up to a whole hog of an audience for companies.

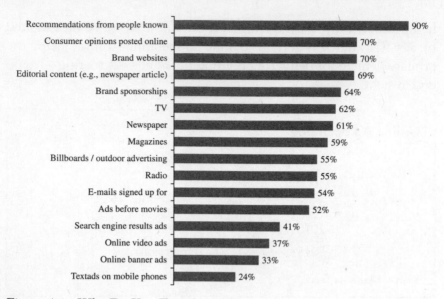

Figure 4.1   Who Do You Trust?

Source: The Nielsen Company.

   Ads range from legitimate (if obnoxious) campaigns that display banners at the top of the web pages you amble onto, to questionable maneuvers that shoot you an unsolicited text or embed a surprise ad inside your mobile app. Then there are downright duplicitous gambits, like company employees who masquerade as consumers on location-based social media sites available via mobile. And do we click on these ads? All the time, often because of their sheer size, often because of their deceptiveness. A 2011 Harris Interactive survey found that mobile users click or tap on ads *by accident* a whopping 47 percent of the time.

2. *Social media.* You probably already have a Facebook and a Twitter account or are pals with someone who does, so I don't have to tell you how engaging this type of communication is. But companies are targeting social media with their promotional dollars. They'll nearly double their investment from 2008 to 2012, when Forrester Research estimates $34 billion will be spent on so-called social media marketing. And while a great many initiatives will be above-board—using only social media to augment and spread

their messages—there are plenty of corporate charlatans working their hardest to deceive customers.

3. *Online videos*. The numbers for online video are equally impressive. Ad spending will nearly quadruple from 2010 to 2014, from $1.5 billion to $5.5 billion, according to projections from market research company eMarketer. Everyone wants to be on YouTube or Vimeo. But when we think of online videos, we don't think ads. We think of adorable kittens on a greeting card site, or Justin Bieber singing *Baby*.

The notion that funny or poignant videos could be ads goes against our instincts. We cling to the extinct model of advertising honesty, and we find it hard to fathom how far companies are now prepared to go to grab our attention—and money. The gold standard is a video that seems to be authentic but that subtly touts a product. In advertising lingo, the video will be shared or go *viral* and is thus seen by tens of millions of people. That's how you get hooked in.

Although some of these initiatives are pretty obvious to the average consumer, the best are undetectable. That means your Facebook friends, Twitter followers, or fellow blog commenters are all suspect. They could be ordinary Janes and Joes, as they claim, or they could be paid shills for a company that wants to enhance its reputation and persuade you to buy a product. Unfortunately, you never know.

How to Find Better Service

One of the most wonderful, but mostly undiscovered, aspects of social media promotion is its ability to meticulously document everything that's happening to you. Here's how: Take a screen shot on your computer. If you're on a PC running on Windows, click PrintScreen. Launch Paint (under Start > All Programs > Accessories), and press the Control V. On a Mac, hold down the Command, Shift, and 4 keys at once to take an immediate copy of your screen. Be sure to save the screenshot somewhere handy. If the promotion is bogus, you have evidence of the shady claim that you can share with the business. Or to give law enforcement.

Pay per Post

Though most of these dissemblers do their dirty work in secret, some have the gall to trumpet their intentions. Here's a job listing I came across:

> We are looking for a few good writers who know their way around Twitter and Facebook who can leave native comments in groups and to people that are relative to our Company's products.
>
> We will pay anyway you like: per comment, per day, per month, per minimum comments left, per forum. Whatever works best for you.

The company goes on to offer between $2 and $5 per comment or forum post "relative to our product." It assures jobseekers that the cash can add up quickly because there are an almost endless number of forums, blogs, and social media outlets.

How to Save Money

The easiest way to tell if something is corporate spin is to *listen*. "Pay attention," says Paul Kurnit, a clinical professor of marketing at Pace University. "If it looks, feels, or sounds like a sales pitch, it probably is." That applies to any message, no matter how trusted the source (in an age of hacked Facebook and Twitter accounts, you can never be sure a message is coming from the sender, anyway). Trust no one. A heavily spun product doesn't necessarily mean it's fraudulent, but it could be a sign of trouble.

Let the Memories Begin

In one video, a little boy dances during a parade at Disney's Magic Kingdom. In another, a young girl dressed as a princess embraces her father. And in a third, two women explore Cinderella Castle.

All are part of Disney's campaign called *Let the Memories Begin*—a promotion that relies on what the company refers to as "guest-generated content."

"*Let the Memories Begin* is about real guests making real memories in our parks," Senior Vice President, Global Marketing, Walt Disney Parks & Resorts Leslie Ferraro told me. "Disney guests have always loved sharing their vacation memories with us and each other. New technologies like YouTube and Facebook have made it easier and faster for our guests to share their memories, for Disney Parks to spotlight those memories on a larger scale, and for us to reinforce to our guests how important we think their memories are."

In 2010, when Disney Parks unveiled the campaign, some experts sniffed it was a "me too" move by Mouseco. But others saw it as an effort to leverage the authenticity of these videos, not the videos themselves. Dancing in a parade, exploring Cinderella Castle, enjoying yourself at the park, are enormous product placements for the Wonderful World and they're using "authentic" production values of home video to drive their message home.

But Wait! There's More!

Now that businesses have broken free from the shackles of traditional advertising, shame takes a backseat. The next time you fly somewhere, you may see an ad on your airline tray table or seatback—or even on the toilet sanitary wraps. Several air carriers already offer these ads, which are literally in your face or on your tush for the duration of your trip.

When you click on the wrong site page, a once-generic error message may be an ad—because shifty marketers know how valuable "Gogle.com" is. This is called 404 marketing, and the most famous case is Burger King's sponsorship of the messages on Digg. Whenever someone clicked on a nonexistent page on Digg.com, they saw a promotional message for the fast-food restaurant instead of an error message.

But perhaps the most egregious cases are ones that take place off-line, if not face-to-face. Most famously, in 2002 Sony Ericsson Mobile hired 60 actors to pose as tourists in New York and Seattle in an effort to demonstrate its T68i mobile phone/digital camera. These fake visitors asked passersby to take their photo, which displayed the camera phone's capabilities; however, the thespians did not identify themselves as Sony representatives and so in effect they were creating a deception.

In 2006, a marketing division of Procter & Gamble assembled a volunteer force of 250,000 teenagers to promote the company's products to friends and relatives. Both these cases prompted regulators to crack down on deceptive word-of-mouth marketing. The government pledged to investigate cases where there was a relationship between an endorser and a seller that wasn't disclosed and could affect the endorsement. Consequences could include a cease-and-desist order, fines, and civil penalties ranging from thousands to millions of dollars.

Rogue marketing like the kind used by Sony and P&G isn't exactly new. In 1929, legendary publicist Edward Bernays, known as the "father of modern PR" (and a nephew of Sigmund Freud), had as his client the huge firm American Tobacco. At this time it was *de rigueur* for a lady to smoke in public—and the tobacco big wanted half the country's business. So Bernays staged a "patriotic" rally to encourage more women to smoke. He secured a list of Manhattan debutantes and invited each one to march in the Easter parade, urging them to wave their symbols of equality, their "torches of freedom"—their cigarettes. Bernays later expressed remorse at promoting an unhealthy product, but not until he was in his late 90s.

What's different now is that many companies never have one afterthought. As long as they can get away with it—and you can be sure that for every company caught, there are thousands that aren't—they'll keep doing it by hook or crook.

As a consumer you probably don't have to be told one fact: When you're fooled into making a purchase, you usually buy the wrong thing. For example, anywhere between 6 and 8 percent of new car owners experience serious buyer's remorse. If just one percentage point of that is due to some form of deceptive marketing—and if those numbers hold true for other industries—then you're talking billions of dollars a year in ill-gotten gains.

If you still think companies are playing fair, you're living in the past. And in denial. Corporations by and large are defying the commonly accepted definition of advertising, forcing corporate messages into every aspect of your life, from the word-of-mouth advice you get from friends to the lyrics of your favorite song. And even updating those advertising messages once they're obsolete. Consider reruns of TV shows like *How I Met Your Mother*, which superimpose ads for *current* movies into billboards as a character walks by them.

Of course there are ways to avoid these surreptitious efforts but they require foresight and diligence. If you don't have these qualities, you can forget about getting a fair shake. As it turns out, the sellers have found a foolproof way to keep your money once you spend it.

5

Lying about Your Rights

If you have ten thousand regulations you destroy all respect for the law.
—Winston Churchill

I'VE BEEN A HAPPY AAA member since 1988 when my late Uncle Clyde helped me buy a used Chevrolet Chevette during my junior year in college. But all that changed one autumn day, when our Honda Accord wouldn't start in the parking lot of my daughter's pre-school. I called the American Automobile Association, as I had done only a few times since becoming a member, and politely requested a tow truck.

"Where are you?" asked the dispatcher.

"I'm at home," I explained. "But my family is with the car."

Too bad, she said. AAA would send a truck over if I were with the vehicle. But since I wasn't, the best they could do was to sell me another membership. (AAA towing applies only to members but doesn't extend to their cars.)

"I can take your credit card number now and process your order," the AAA representative told me with more than a little smugness.

What she meant to say was, "Give us $30, or your family suffers. And by the way, didn't you read the fine print in your agreement?"

51

Actually, I hadn't since joining AAA more than 20 years ago.

It seemed like a small issue, but was it? You'd be bowled over by all the snares lurking in many of the contracts you sign with allegedly reputable companies. Agreements are often phrased in ways that have one overriding purpose: to strip you of any means of redress in potential quarrels over a product or service. The authors of these nearly useless documents conceal gotchas behind what appear to be prominently disclosed and reasonable terms. They're called in-house lawyers, and they're paid by the year, not the hour.

Even Triple A, which is a nonprofit company, has fine print that would make any self-respecting contract attorney proud. For example, AAA South (of which I was a member) lists numerous benefits for prospective members on its wordy site. But its terms and conditions then pour cold water on those promises:

There is no warranty that any information or service provided or referenced by this site is either merchantable or accurate, that such information or service will fulfill any of your particular purposes or needs, or that such information or service does not infringe on any third party rights.

Got it? Didn't think so.

AAA is basically saying it's not responsible for the accuracy of any product or service it offers. What's more, the terms say that if I have a dispute, I have to sue it in Tampa, even if I live hundreds of miles away, which is called a venue clause (more on that in a bit).

Contracts like AAA's are known as adhesion agreements because they bind or "adhere to" only one of two parties: the consumer. And AAA's adhesion clause is tame compared to those compiled by the legal eagles of for-profit businesses, which are sugarcoated with seductive promises while allotting you no rights at all. But few customers have the patience to wade through all that verbiage and are trapped by the conditions the moment they click "I accept" after downloading software or by even opening a box. (Also, never cash a check until you read the memo line—it could stop you from getting what is due.)

Aside from the intimidating lengths of some of these agreements, the fine print would challenge even the sharpest didacts; microprint can be very fine. For example it takes about an hour to read through the Apple iTunes end-user license agreement, EULA (not skimming—actually reading). According to a poll conducted by antivirus software provider Lavasoft, 63 percent of people accept these EULAs without first reading them—which is too bad. If they reviewed them, here's what they'd find:

- *Forced arbitration clauses.* Nearly all contracts offered by credit card companies and many bank loans, mortgages, and phone companies have clauses that require you to use an arbitrator if you have a dispute instead of going to court. Unfortunately, only 4 percent of consumers prevail in arbitration.
- *Forum selection clauses.* This language restricts the place where you can seek legal relief. Often, it's as bad as a forced arbitration clause because it means you have to travel long distances to a higher court or a maritime court (if you're taking a cruise) to sue a company.
- *Restrictive terms.* These gotchas can include just about anything you can imagine, from alarm companies that sell you a cheap system but force you into a multiyear contract to credit cards that automatically adjust to a sky-high interest rate after a certain amount of time has elapsed.
- *Acceleration clauses.* An acceleration clause in a contract requires that you pay the entire remaining balance of installment payments in the event of a default. For example, if you miss a monthly car payment, an acceleration clause would require you to pay for the car in full. Credit cards also use acceleration clauses to raise interest rates. Such clauses can financially devastate a consumer.

And, according to a *South Park* episode, there is an umpteenth clause: Apple has the right to take you from your house and use your body for experiments.

The net result is that you think you're getting a good deal—like a low interest rate credit card or a membership in an auto club that guarantees you and your vehicle will never be abandoned—but you're getting an empty promise, or worse, one that's booby-trapped throughout.

> ## Not Every Arbitration Clause Holds Up in Court
>
> In 2006, the virtual game *Second Life* terminated lawyer Marc Bragg's account because he had figured out a way to acquire "virtual" land at below-market prices. Like any good lawyer, Bragg sued *Second Life*. Though the company's EULA had a mandatory arbitration clause, the court refused to enforce it; it argued that the contract was a one-sided, take-it-or-leave-it agreement that Bragg had essentially been forced to sign if he wanted to participate in *Second Life*. The case was settled out of court, and *Second Life* changed its contract in response.

Oops, You've Already Signed It

Don't look now, but you've probably already signed one of these egregious contracts. How? You are guilty just by opening a product's plastic wrap or clicking on its website.

A *shrinkwrap contract*, common on many computer software purchases, is a notice inside the box that says you agree to the terms within simply by opening it. Never mind the fact that you didn't have an opportunity to review the terms before agreeing to them; the terms are more often punitive than principled. For example, one computer manufacturer had a provision in one of its shrinkwrap agreements that required users with a claim against the company to agree to arbitration—but not before paying a $4,000 fee, half of which was nonrefundable. Thankfully, a court refused to enforce the clause.

A *clickwrap*, or *clickthrough*, agreement is the virtual equivalent of a shrinkwrap contract. It's usually found on the Internet when installing software or visiting a site. Typically, users have the opportunity to click through to a contract that can be read online; however, most just click Accept and continue. But maybe you should take the opportunity to read the contract. In 2009, the Federal Trade Commission alleged that retail giant Sears hid a provision in its clickwrap agreement to install what amounted to spyware on customers' computers. The application stored information about all the sites participants visited and the complete text of secure pages—including, gasp!, online banking statements, video rental transactions, library borrowing histories, online prescription records, and header fields that showed the sender, recipients, and subjects of e-mails. Sears settled with the government quickly.

Another sneaky agreement: the *sign-without-reading* contract. Why would consumers sign a contract they haven't read? Because they're told they don't need to. And since the paperwork is loaded with ridiculous amounts of fine print, you trust the synopsis offered to you orally or via pamphlet. I find this is common across many industries, from home contractors to office equipment leases to financial services products. "Just sign here," a smiling agent tells you—and later when you have a problem you realize you've waived many of your rights.

Many contracts can *change without notice.* Unbelievable, right? Companies reserve the right to alter the terms at any time for any reason and sometimes without any notification. Consider the dust-up after cloud-storage service Dropbox slipped a clause in its terms of service that said it would turn your files over to the government if asked. Such a provision is common in other cloud services' contracts, including Gmail, Hotmail, and Amazon cloud. But Dropbox's promises contradict earlier statements that suggest even its own employees can't access your account. And this kind of contract updating is a lot more common than you might think. You've probably received several notifications from your credit card in the last year notifying you of rate changes or new conditions or even privacy "changes." Chances are, it wasn't written in English but rather legalese; even more likely, you tossed it into the garbage without reading it—which is exactly what these companies want you to do.

How to Save Money

There is only one proven way to protect yourself from these onerous contracts: Say "no way." If a box pops up on your screen that demands you accept terms that you don't like, just refuse. And let the company know you won't do it. If representatives hand you a brochure about your benefits but withhold the paperwork, stop

(continued)

(*continued*)

them cold. Demand to see the agreement. Saying "no way" is the only way to ensure companies change how they do business. It could save you from costly mistakes. The alternative "yeah sure" saves time that is rightly valuable, but in the long term saying "no way" saves you the bucks.

Fine Print Gone Wild

One of the most outrageous examples of fine print involves the wily world of loyalty programs. Airlines, hotels, coffee places, and most other companies promise you the world, like free flights, upgrades, and hotel stays, but the contracts often say otherwise.

Rachel Cabarcas and her spouse were loyal Southwest Airlines frequent fliers but hadn't had as much of a chance to travel when they contacted me. They'd been saving their hard-earned frequent flier credits for a vacation with their young daughter. Yet when they logged on to the airline's site they discovered that four of their credits had vanished. "I just want to be able to use them," Cabarcas pleaded with me via e-mail. "Please help."

Southwest's program rules at the time claimed its vouchers expire if there's no activity in an account, but that wasn't the only kick in the head. A closer look at Southwest's terms for its unfortunately named Rapid Rewards program reveals it can do anything it wants with your points.

For example, the airline "reserves the right to amend, suspend, terminate, or change, with 30 days notice, the Terms and Conditions of the program, including but not limited to changing the points and Award levels, adding or deleting Partners, changing the terms for use of the Award at any time, and modifying or terminating the program." Which means it's worthless. Your miles don't belong to you, and they can be taken away whenever the airline feels like it. And for the record, that is the industry standard.

So I connected Cabarcas with a high-level Southwest manager who begrudgingly bent a rule and gave the family two-thirds of their miles back—which would help them get most of the way to their destination, Florida. "Something's better than nothing, right?" she says. Yes it is.

Signing Away Other Rights

Watch what you sign at a doctor's office. A company called Medical Justice has been trying to address the issue of what it calls web defamation by asking patients to sign mutual agreements with doctors that gives physicians who believe they've received an unfairly negative online review the tools to remove it.

The agreement exploits a loophole in the controversial 1997 Communications Decency Act (CDA), which protects online free speech and was developed when the commercial web was still in grade school. If a review is false or defamatory, the CDA has found a way to protect both the commenter and the forum where it's posted.

However, the Medical Justice agreement has used the CDA in a way that has riled politicians for years. It claims that any review written by a patient is copyrighted material—and the CDA treats intellectual property differently. So if a forum gets a takedown notice for copyrighted material, it almost always complies by removing the review immediately.

Clever by half, right? Perhaps too smart for its own good. A group of legal scholars called Doctored Reviews dismisses Medical Justice's reasoning as nonsense. The contracts help neither patients nor doctors, but Medical Justice denies it is trying to stifle free speech and wants to encourage "honest online feedback." I'm troubled—and you should be, too—by the potential for Medical Justice's legal logic to disrupt the free flow of information on the Internet. Imagine if other companies followed suit. You might actually be required to censor yourself and refrain from posting opinions about the raw deal you got at a car wash or a burger stand.

One Word at a Time

Businesses are taking away a customer's rights one word at a time. Whether it's a relatively small privilege (ability to sue in your local venue) or a bigger one (the freedom to speak up and offer your opinion about shoddy service), it is being removed slowly, quietly, and without consumer knowledge.

We've just taken a hard look at how companies scam their customers by ruthlessly managing their online reputations, manipulating search engines, making slippery product claims, concealing advertising messages, and limiting your rights through onerous contracts. I've also shown how these corporate shenanigans can cost far more than the traditional lowercase scams, since they evade detection under legal guises and are able to ensnare far more victims.

But none of this could work without the help of that one unknowing participant, namely you.

Now I'll show how we have all become complicit in these schemes, swindles, and shady deals.

How We Scam Ourselves

6

Our Own Damned Fault

Don't find fault, find a remedy.

—Henry Ford

DURING THE SUMMER of 1987, my friend Steve and I were unemployed, living with my grandmother in Southern California, and eager to find jobs to cover our college tuition bills. As we pulled into the parking lot of a grocer's one blazing hot Saturday afternoon, a man approached us and asked if we wanted to buy a color television. It was brand-spanking new, still in the box, and would cost us just $40.

Quicker than you could say "Yes," two $20 bills had passed from our two wallets into his hands while a box in brown packaging passed to us. He warned, "Don't open it here, man," with his eyes darting side to side. "We don't want anyone to see this."

So, obediently, we waited until we got home and opened the package to find one thing for sure: That salesman was right that the TV was new—once. But today it was garbage—a nonfunctioning, burnt-out piece of cleverly repackaged junk. Forty bucks for a dumpster pick! And that was a quarter century ago when $40 actually bought something.

We kicked ourselves.

I still kick myself when I think about it (I'm doing it now—ouch!). Once I brushed off the event as youthful naïveté, but when I became a consumer advocate, I knew better. Age has nothing to do with it. Steve and I could have been scammed anytime and not because today's conmen are so much more sophisticated with their tactics. It's because every one of us wants to believe in too-good-to-be-true. We do this to *ourselves*.

A great deal of research on what is known as consumer vulnerability focuses on the measurable influences that lead a person to make a purchase—external variables like the item's price or characteristics like age, race, gender, and income. And there are certainly some undeniable influences that can make you a target for a rip-off. For example, if I'd been a 39-year-old, perhaps I wouldn't have fallen for the fake TV scam. I probably wouldn't have been there during the day, between jobs, and with a friend. In the unlikely event I had been approached, the scammer wouldn't have had a chance.

But I still might fall for a fraudulent or semi-real fractional ownership offer while on a scuba-diving vacation in Cancun, Mexico. If an attractive saleswoman bought me a round of margaritas, as timeshare pushers are wont to do, and invited me to a "brief" sales presentation, the 39-year-old me might drop $50,000 on a condo I would never use, and from which I'd never see my money again.

How to Save Money

You know the adage: "If it's too good to be true, it probably is"? It's too simplistic to apply to every consumer choice. That's because some things seem too good to be true, but *are*. They include free e-mail (Gmail or Hotmail) and certain food deals (99 cent Big Macs—how do they make any money off that? Expensive French fries!). Instead of shrugging off the deal, try this: If after careful consideration you believe it would be impossible for a business to make a real profit on an offer, then I'll bet you a bridge in Brooklyn that it's fraudulent. Avoid such offers and save money and headaches.

Consumers aren't just a *part of* the scam problem; sometimes, they *are* the problem. Research suggests we're influenced by instincts and subconscious desires that we haven't come to understand. By failing to cast a critical eye on products and neglecting to do basic math on the price of certain services, we invite unsavory offers upon ourselves. And then we proudly make a purchase. Marketers know we don't think before we act, and no society before us has, so the smartest among them promote products accordingly, targeting our unconscious mind with pitches to which we can't say no.

Losing Your Mind

Here's a fairly obvious question: Have we lost our marbles when it comes to being responsible? Answer: a resounding yes.

- Research more than suggests that consumers do less thinking than acting before making a purchasing decision and are often unaware of the forces that dictate behavior. A Yale study indicates that capuchin monkeys share some of our basic economic decision-making processes, which must make you feel great. This leads scientists to conclude that we make many consumer choices purely by instinct. In other words, we're hardwired to do stupid things when we ponder a purchase.
- For example, instead of returning a luxury item that doesn't match the rest of a home's décor, customers in a University of Houston study went the *other* way: They purchased even more unaffordable items to make the out-of-place item look at home. (This is the nonhumorous version of the woman who buys an entire outfit, a handbag, and loads of accessories to match new shoes.) Oh, and it gets even juicier: Some people will purchase a *new home* to make the "off" furniture come across better. Researchers even have a name for this ill-advised emotional response: aesthetic incongruity resolution. Say that five times quickly.
- What's worse is we don't learn from our mistakes and we tend to repeat them. We are frequently unaware of the forces conspiring in our heads to make bad decisions and therefore can't help ourselves. It's largely a function of brain chemistry that is triggered by

cleverly placed decoys, as author Dan Ariely explains in his groundbreaking 2008 book, *Predictably Irrational: The Hidden Forces That Shape Our Decisions*.

But you don't have to be a scientist or an academic to know people enact bad buying behavior. How often have you come home to a loved one who didn't just make a questionable purchasing decision but one that is so off the charts you are speechless? You know, the rhinestone-studded jacket that was on sale (two for one, naturally) but that the buyer will never wear. Or a frivolous item like one more unnecessary big-screen TV, or a trampoline, or a two-level juicer, or . . . you get the idea. If this has occurred in your home, or by you, then you know the feeling. Rational creature you may be, but something happened between your doorstep and the shopping mall and now you own a tree-shaped lava lamp.

Truth is, we are not rational most of the time; it's just not our makeup. Studies suggest there's a sea of impulses and instincts of which we're completely unaware and way below our conscious mind, *Twilight Zone*–like forces that drive us without our knowing it to make strange, unfortunate, unreasonable purchasing decisions. These forces control our purse strings. It's like *Night of the Living Wallet*! We can't hope to fully understand what is happening in the little pockets of our brains; all we can do is become aware of our behavior.

Luckily, we can control what is happening aboveground, and here's where the discussion turns practical. All right, so maybe you aren't aware that your inner child is jumping up and down when it sees the bright orange FOR SALE sign that insists you buy the diamond unisex brooch. But there's an abundance of anecdotal evidence suggesting that consumers give in to their impulses and simply stop thinking critically. The eye that makes decisions has gone blind—and we've stopped being concerned with being good consumers.

Take the problem of financial illiteracy, which is a huge issue in our nation. As I write this, we're still fighting our way out of the worst recession since the 1930s—one brought on by a collective mania to make boneheaded financial decisions. For many years economists Annamaria Lusardi and Olivia Mitchell have studied the problem of financial literacy, or our inability to make rational decisions about money. As part of their research, Lusardi and Mitchell gave a

> **Beware of Door-to-Door Scammers**
>
> Sometimes your own common sense can be short-circuited by a slick salesman who shows up at your front door—that is, if you open your door. A survey by Canadian polling company Angus Reid found the following facts about door-to-door purchases:
>
> - Fifty-eight percent felt pressured into making a purchase or signing a contract.
> - Sixty-one percent who bought something experienced buyer's remorse and regretted signing a contract.
> - Seventy percent felt angry about getting burned at the door.

representative sample of Americans over age 50 a quiz. (Sample question: "Imagine that the interest rate on your savings account was 1 percent per year and inflation was 2 percent per year. After one year would you be able to buy more than, exactly the same as, or less than today with the money in this account?") Only half the respondents were able to figure out the obvious answer: "less than."

Most efforts to improve our financial education are not at all effective, says New York University business professor Thomas Cooley. The very thing that nearly led to the collapse of the world economy—our ignorance, greed, and inability to comprehend real-time occurrence of both—could occur again. It doesn't help that financial product companies have cultivated our collective dumbness with soothing slogans and confusing product offers. But the sad fact is, we let them. And how.

A Scam-or-Be-Scammed World?

Maybe I'm exaggerating when I say consumers brought all of this upon themselves. But unlike the conventional wisdom of the twentieth century—that customers are just victims that need our help—the modern truth is a little more nuanced, and a lot more troubling.

We live in a world where you can buy a laptop computer for $100 and a video camera for less than $40, and in which our mobile handsets (yeah, even smartphones) are free—as long as you sign a usurious agreement. And we seem to like that abuse. As Ellen Shell observed in her fascinating 2009 book *Cheap: The High Cost of Discount Culture*, scientists now see that the very *anticipation* of a bargain "sets our neural networks aquiver." Low prices confuse us and "ignite the impulsive, primitive side, the part that leads us to make poor decisions based on bad assumptions," she notes.

We are, once again, as big a part of the problem as those who sell these horrid products. Here are my favorite examples:

There's Something in the VitaminWater

The setup. If you're looking for a healthy alternative to sugary soda, why not grab a VitaminWater? With flavors like "energy," "revive," and "multi-v" you can even feel good about giving this beverage to your kids. Sure, VitaminWater can cost twice as much as its bubbly counterpart, but it's good for you, because this "Nutrient Enhanced Water Beverage" contains nothing more than "vitamins + water," which is "all you need."

The scam. A 2009 suit against Coca-Cola, which owns the company that produces VitaminWater, alleges the drink doesn't consist solely of "vitamins + water". Rather, it contains 33 grams of sugar, which is almost as much sugar as contained in a can of Coke. Coca-Cola's claims about the health benefits of VitaminWater are "false, misleading, deceptive, and unfair," according to the suit. In fact, it's just another flavored, sugary snack food like Coca-Cola. The only difference between VitaminWater and soda pop? VitaminWater isn't carbonated.

The spin. In 2010, Coca-Cola tried to dismiss the case, calling the suit "ridiculous" and saying the claims against it were mere "puffery." But a federal judge in New York was unpersuaded, and the case is still alive.

How we asked for it. Consumers' demand for "healthy" drinks seems to be unquenchable. Sales of VitaminWater are half a billion dollars a year and growing, for example. But we aren't so good with details. Check the label of a VitaminWater, and you'll see that it contains 50 calories per 8-ounce serving. That's about 6 calories per fluid ounce, which is about half the calorie count of regular Coke. But

VitaminWater comes in a 20-ounce bottle, which ratchets up the calorie count for one bottle to 125 calories. Do thirsty consumers bother to study the tricky label? Hardly.

A Wayward Offer from DirecTV

The setup. Want to discover the DirecTV difference? There's no equipment and no start-up costs, and for only $29.99, you can get all of your favorite TV shows. It's a pitch that has scored DirecTV hundreds of thousands of subscribers, making it the nation's largest satellite provider. With the implied promise of a low price, no-strings-attached offer, and hundreds of channels to choose from, who wouldn't want to make the switch?

The scam. A lawsuit filed by the state of Washington alleged the $29 offer is complete nonsense and that DirecTV has "built deception into its business model." Specifically, what was *not* disclosed to prospective customers was an onerous early termination fee. A particularly lie-filled marketing campaign spoke of service for $29.99 per month but glossed over the two-year obligation or the teensy fact that the price of service doubled after the first year, or so the suit alleged. In 2010 the case was settled and the company agreed to a $1 million fine. DirecTV now discloses the terms, albeit in really small type. (Maybe its next ad campaign will be "DirecTV with inDirectPricing!")

The spin. The satellite conglomerate, which is locked in a brutal fight for TV dominance with cable, Dish, and the telcos, wasted no time here and launched a forceful initiative to counter the allegations brought herein. Suddenly, conventional damage control and unconventional reputation management came out with teeth. A little sleuthing revealed some of its off-the-books efforts—which included populating blogs with a whole lot of positive comments; attempting to bury anything negative online; and pressuring critics to remove embarrassing content from websites.

How we asked for it. Who has the time to read fine print? But the devil is in the details, and when enough customers ignore the paperwork, bad-acting types like DirecTV add increasingly restrictive terms to their agreements, and we are none the wiser. A company may even consider this tendency on the part of consumers as a license to tell a lie or two, thereby taking Shortcut Lane to Profitville. It takes both vigilance by consumers *and* executives with a strong moral compass to resist the temptation.

That's Not the Spirit

The setup. If you want a cheap airfare from New York to Florida or the Caribbean, Spirit Airlines may offer just what you're looking for—at your first glance. The airline, whose prices are uniformly low, has roundtrip deals to Florida for $49. Other air carriers, like Allegiant Air, hawk similar deals to hot destinations like Vegas, baby.

The scam. These fares are a barely legal bait-and-switch; once the airline adds boarding pass printing fees, checked luggage, carry-on luggage (I wish I were kidding), and a "seat reservation" charge to your total, a $49 fare can double and sometimes triple. Oh, and Allegiant has the gall to charge a "convenience" fee to use your credit card, which borders on illegal. So you won't pay the published fare—*ever*. This is like going to a movie that the ad says starts at "7:40 P.M." and expecting the credits to begin rolling at 7:40 P.M. In the case of this spirited airline, and others like it, a lobbying group calling themselves Open Allies for Airfare Transparency is fighting the trend of quoting a theoretical base fare, "which has brought in billions of dishonest dollars to the airline industry and has turned countless passengers against the industry as a whole."

The spin. Just hours after announcing what has to be the most controversial ancillary fee to date—the carry-on luggage charge—Spirit CEO Ben Baldanza gave his first exclusive interview to me, in which he acknowledged the vital role of online reputation management. Baldanza later appeared on several morning talkers and network news shows to defend the fees. The airline's efforts to control its reputation have been irreverent, to say the least. Its online campaigns have pushed the boundaries of good taste, frequently using sexual innuendo—which gets more clicks and pushes search results higher—to drown out the huge number of critics. At least he's not charging for the bathroom—yet.

How we asked for it. For years the majority of air travelers have told airlines via surveys and how they purchase tickets that they care only about low fares and nothing else matters. Airlines finally took a page from wireless carriers and started stripping away everything but the basic rate in order to make their prices look extra attractive. Now you need a calculator to figure out how much a flight really costs. Often, it's already too late, and we've bought the overpriced ticket with no recourse except to pay a cancellation or change fee. Remarkably, despite their anger, customers come back for more abuse from the high-flyers.

Why does this keep happening? According to Jason Goldberg, a vice president of strategy for e-commerce company CrossView, we make purchase decisions in our brains, and the overwhelming majority of these are influenced by factors we have no control over. "Often our conscious brain is then called upon to rationally justify the decision our subconscious brain has already made," Goldberg says.

The cleverest marketers are aware of this so they try to understand the way your brain tries to persuade itself it's made a right decision. Once you see how to do that you can make the sale. "You can change the external inputs that your brain gets and have a dramatic effect on the purchase decisions that are made," adds Goldberg.

For example, let's say that you're at the mall. You walk into a store with a large assortment of shoes clumsily piled up in boxes. Your brain assumes the shoes are priced competitively—with this kind of decoration they have to be cheap. But when you see a lone pair of the same shoes in a boutique, bathed in theatrical lighting, you automatically think, "Gosh, those *have* to be expensive!" According to Goldberg, "Your subconscious brain is taking a shortcut to save you cognitive energy."

Marketing like this figures out a way to make you *think* you've found a bargain without saying a word. And it doesn't matter whether it's an actual bargain or a rip-off. Your unconscious mind decides for you.

To get an idea of how an unconscious decision is made, consider this quiz given by neuroscientist Dean Buonomano in his 2011 book *Brain Bugs: How the Brain's Flaws Shape Our Lives.* Answer the following questions: (1) What continent is Kenya in? (2) What are the two opposing colors in the game of chess? (3) Name any animal. If you said "zebra," then you have something in common with 20 percent of those who took the same quiz. But without two previous questions, less than 1 percent mentioned a zebra. By directing your attention to

Africa and the colors black and white, the quiz manipulated you into a certain answer. Buonomano calls this priming, and it's something marketers do all the time, triggering the "buy" impulse with various stimuli.

Consumers also use experience-based techniques for learning and discovery—something known as heuristics—to guide them when they're at the store. We have, you see, been conditioned to think of past performance as an indicator of future returns. The fact that we can automate certain cognitive processes makes us more efficient; it's wonderful how we've evolved this way as humans. But as consumers, this can be a hindrance. Why? Because stores have learned that people can get the feeling of buying at a good price by purchasing an item from the bargain rack or even by buying in bulk without checking whether that feeling is borne out by a single fact. Retailers can leverage our collective experiences and have a grand old time playing around with profit margins that meet their ends.

Another questionable tactic used by businesses is offering only a few genuine discounts on products for which customers know the cost and letting shoppers presume everything around it is a bargain when in fact these could be more expensive than any competitor sells them for.

Customer Confessions

You've probably said one of the following phrases at some point. The good news is, I can explain why you said them—and soon I'll help you learn to stop saying them and make smarter purchases.

- *"I don't know which one I want!"* Indecision is not a customer's fault. Go to any big box store, and you'll find you're overwhelmed with choice paralysis. Research shows that more choices make it more difficult—and even painful—to arrive at a purchasing decision. Although that may be a bad kind of indecision, at least it's one in which you're attempting to come to a conclusion. What's worse is approaching a decision as a consumer and not knowing what you want *at all*. Such customers are at their most vulnerable state when they are clueless—and that kind of internal indecision is never frowned upon in our "charrrrge it!" culture. It is celebrated.

■ *"I'm in a hurry!"* Because time is precious in this always-on world, customers often make choices without considering the consequences. It's true that with some decisions the quicker the better, as Malcolm Gladwell suggests in his 2005 book, *Blink: The Power of Thinking without Thinking.* Even some consumer decisions we make with zero thought will turn out right, according to newer research. But snap decisions like buying the first house you see or the first car you test can really lead to disastrous consequences. Generally speaking, you need to think before you buy.

■ *"I didn't shop around!"* No one knows how many customers comparison-shop before deciding on a purchase; estimates range from half to more than 90 percent. The best-case scenario is that roughly 5 percent of Americans don't bother to do any research. I suspect the number is higher (at least half of us don't comparison-shop; think back to your last gas purchase if you doubt me).

I've dealt with more than my fair share of customers who failed to shop, and instead made an impulse buy or shelled out perfectly green money for something without one iota of thought. Businesses love these nincompoops because the same people fail to ask other crucial questions like "What's in the fine print?" Indeed, one 2010 survey by mortgage company Lending Tree found that less than half comparison-shopped for a mortgage, arguably one of the most important purchases ever.

■ *"I don't care so long as it works!"* Apathy plagues today's consumer like no other emotion. You know you care about some aspects of spending more than others. For example, you might review your credit card statement regularly, but do you read your utility bills with the same eye? A British survey found that two-thirds of mobile phone customers hadn't taken the time to read what service plan they had chosen and one in five respondents felt they had the wrong plan (uh, how would they conclude that if they hadn't read which one?). The "I-don't-care-as-long-as-it-works" attitude is so pervasive that hardly anyone notices it exists.

Marketing experts think they've won you over before you even set foot in their stores or log on to their sites. Philadelphia-based Center for Cultural Studies & Analysis—a well-known think tank that studies human behavior—researches how we make decisions. Its in-house study, "The Artemis Project" (after the huntress in Greek mythology), looks at those innate behaviors driving shopping behavior.

"Our core findings," says Director Margaret King, "demonstrate that *all* buy decisions are pre-sold—even if the buyer doesn't know that they are in the market."

Let's look at cars. Research shows that people start noticing new auto ads about nine months before they report being in the market for wheels. The unconscious mind made the decision long before their conscious awareness found out. In between those two events the unconscious took action—searching the landscape, making choices and cuts, narrowing the target list—all before the buyer was aware he was thinking about a new one! "By the time consumers start making conscious choices, the field has been narrowed to two or three models—out of a possible three thousand," says King. "The best marketing can tap into the pre-existing demand at the right time in the process and with the correct cues to value. If this is done right, the unconscious will put the product into the top choice basket for the conscious process to sort out."

Companies think they have us exactly where they want us. We're careless, we're apathetic, and research shows that our subconscious minds are making most, if not all, the important decisions. The only way to stop bad behavior is to become aware of it. But waking up isn't as simple as it sounds.

7

Walled Gardens

If you look for truth, you may find comfort in the end; if you look for comfort you will not get either comfort or truth only soft soap and wishful thinking to begin, and in the end, despair.

—C.S. Lewis

ON AN OPPRESSIVELY humid day in June 2007, an Apple store lured me into the cool shade of its walled garden. I'd been standing outside the building for several hours, waiting in a long line to buy a shiny new iPhone—and when I finally paid more than $500 for mine, I wasn't disappointed. The multimedia device was sleekly intuitive and beautiful.

Unfortunately, it was also a trap. Not only did I sign a burdensome contract with AT&T—the only authorized wireless provider at that point—but the device itself was also highly restrictive. Its operating system was designed to run only applications approved by the parent company (Apple) and only those that carried the company's cryptographic signature, a snippet of code that authenticates the program. If I ever left Apple's garden, I risked voiding my warranty—or who knows what else.

A "walled garden" is an environment that controls your access to content and services. Apple's app store and the iTunes program are just two examples. AOL and Facebook are among the most famous walled gardens of our time; and to some extent the paywalls of media organizations like the *Wall Street Journal* or the *New York Times* are as well. But there are other de facto walled gardens where we find ourselves every day without even realizing it: places we're made to feel cozy as consumers and where it's all so easy, but where unseen obstacles make critical decision-making impossible.

These gardens don't just make the businesses that control almost everything we see and do more profitable; customers seem to enjoy being in them. As Apple's former CEO Steve Jobs told a tech conference in 2010, a "curated" app store is the nearest thing to Nirvana for consumers, who don't have to deal with cheaters or porn peddlers. And walled gardens have a standard look, so once you're inside them you're more comfortable because the environment is familiar to you. (Could anyone go for a Starbucks latte right about now?) Mostly customers like having the security of a walled garden because it keeps out spam and the bad guys—who doesn't want that?

But what are you giving up for that comfort? Well, Apple's app store is famously controlling, forcing developers to use only Apple-authorized tools to develop software. It won't allow them to use Adobe Flash technology for rendering graphic animation; Apple feels that HTML5 is the better tool, and they're sure you will, too. It imposes limits on users that strike me as somewhat harsh, including those on how apps that you buy can be shared between devices and users. This attitude seems draconian. Apple's iTunes program is notoriously restrictive, preventing users from copying movies they purchased onto a DVD or easily sharing songs across computers ("your limit is five"). Spend enough time in Apple's walled garden, and you might feel as though you're in prison. In his book, *The Future of the Internet—and How to Stop It*, Jonathan Zittrain maintains such closed systems are bad for society—and innovation.

Apple got it right; make something easy and safe, and consumers will choose it over something more open but riskier. Jobs, who claims to avoid market research and focus groups, would be the first to point to Apple's astounding success since 2001 as evidence of collective risk aversion. Maybe we're so tempted by gardens because they replicate the safety we want in real life. Haven't we shown a resounding appreciation for shopping malls, those real-life walled gardens? Think about malls (*sans* Kevin James). They offer a variety of shops under one roof in a clean, well-maintained environment. These little societies also control exactly which vendors can set up shop—and how long they can stay open, and on what days, and how their storefronts must appear, and so on and so forth—not unlike what Apple does on iTunes and in the app store, or Facebook does with everything it controls. If you think about it, we started it; today there are more than 7 billion square feet of shopping center space on earth.

Shopping Malls in the United States	
1922	1
1964	7,600
1972	13,174
2009	105,000

Source: International Council of Shopping Centers.

But malls are a by-product of something much more insidious: the abdication of the American consumer's responsibility to become an informed shopper. By preferring the easiness of malls—and more recently the vanilla of the big box stores—we've sacrificed choice for convenience and forfeited any role as critics. We've paid a dear price for it. Closed systems are now a centerpiece of the economy; whether it's obvious (like a proprietary computer operating system or program) or less apparent (like the malls we get lost in), I think it's only a matter of time until someone tells us exactly where and when we can shop all the time.

So how do walled gardens hurt us? Let me count the ways.

1. *They limit choice*. Closed systems make comparison shopping really difficult, if not impossible. A "curated" space like a mall or an app store—like ones on Amazon.com or BlackBerry—can exclude anyone it wants to, which is fairly discriminatory and limits the

options you have as a customer. I know that *more* choices are not always better, but if the curators have that much power, how do you know if they have your best interests at heart? You don't, particularly when they mostly answer to shareholders.

2. *They charge more*. Whether it's the retailer jacking up prices to cover rent or the software developer naming his price because the competition is nil, we know closed systems are costlier. For example, 34 cents of every 99 cent song downloaded from iTunes goes to Apple. Take away the iTunes equation, and music labels could offer the same songs for two-thirds of the price. (I believe the opportunity for that never occurred to them, though.) You cannot argue with the logic that walls drive prices higher.

3. *They stand in the way of serious progress*. A lot of walled gardens seem appealing because they make life simple. But what if they were open? What if Apple allowed Flash or if Facebook didn't hide most of its content behind password-protected areas? What if Microsoft's operating system were open source and let programmers see what made the platform tick? The outcome would be more innovation—which would benefit consumers in both choice and price.

4. *You give more than you get*. This is particularly true of the Internet's walled gardens. Sure, you get to interact with your friends in a safe environment, but you also have to surrender a significant amount of personal information—data that you wouldn't dream of offering a stranger you *liked*. That decision can come back to haunt you when a walled garden decides to change its terms of service or suffers a security breach, releasing your personal information to unknown parties. (This happens a lot. Who can forget the security breach at retailer T.J. Maxx, which exposed information from more than 45 million credit and debit cards to hackers back in 2007? Worst of all, the company didn't reveal the full extent of the breach until two months *after* the electronic break-in.)

5. *They make you lazy and apathetic*. Customers who frequent walled gardens get comfortable. They tend not to comparison shop, they pay whatever they're told to, and are often unaware of shopping opportunities outside the prison, uh, I mean, *garden* walls. The confines make the consumers complacent and less critical when

A Walled Garden Horror Story

Here's a story about a company that couldn't survive within the confines of a walled garden. It is a true tale that proves that its failure deprived its innovative product to hundreds of thousands of consumers. The iFlowReader, an e-book app for the iPhone and iPad, sold inside Apple's app store. In 2011, Apple announced it would charge a 30 percent tax on new subscriptions sold through its store and declared without explanation that publishers could not include links to external sites where content or subscriptions could be purchased outside the app store.

Publishers were outraged by what they called an arbitrary and heavy-handed move by Apple, and iFlowReader stopped selling e-books via Apple. The 30 percent cut sadly wouldn't cut it for them. "Unfortunately, because of the 'agency model' that has been adopted by the largest publishers, our gross margin on e-books after paying the wholesaler is less than 30 percent, which means that we would have to take a loss on all ebooks sold," the company told readers. "This is not . . . sustainable."

On May 31, 2011, the iFlowReader was shuttered. "Apple changed the rules and put us out of business," it said on its site. Shortly after that, Apple reversed its rule, allowing in-app subscriptions under pressure (and name-calling in the press) but too late for iFlowReader.

How to Save Money

Here's a favorite piece of advice you'll hear from consumer advocates: If something seems easy, you're being scammed. This has a special application for the walled gardens of the world. If a process is so straightforward that you can't believe how simple it was—like paying with a credit card or signing up for a new service—then red flags should be flapping in the wind. Walled gardens try to make everything look *so* easy. Taking your money will be just as easy for the company that's ripping you off.

Signs You're in a Walled Garden

Closed, walled, proprietary—doesn't matter what you call it. You want to be aware when you're doing business in one. But how can you tell? Consider:

- *Is it easy?* Walled gardens make the process seamless and simple. For example, Amazon.com may not have the best prices or even the largest selection of merchandise, but buying is a cinch with its patented "1-Click" technology that lets you purchase something with a single mouse click. For a while its slogan was "Amazon. And You're Done." (Or done for!)
- *Is making a decision painless?* The best of the walled gardens don't challenge you when it comes to decision making. If you want a bite to eat at the mall, head to the food court— it's the only game in mall-town. There's only one movie theater with multiple screens and a limited selection of anchor stores on the perimeter. That makes shopping easy—*too* easy—and a little *Stepford*, too. (You know, the perfect-wives-are-actually-androids kind of easy.)
- *Is there any real competition?* Closed systems have little or nothing to compete against. The rulebook in a mall is heavy: no two stores can be alike or sell items that might be on par with the other. The prices are uniform (in iTunes, $.99 or $1.29 per song) and quite arbitrary, and you don't have more than one choice of product. In Amazon.com's case, the "world's biggest bookstore" only sells Kindle e-books, because it sells the Kindle e-reader. However, there are many different formats of books—and "world's biggest" couldn't care less. Any "competition" that might indeed exist within the system is heavily restricted. It's like a planned community of sellers with their arms folded.

they should be on their guard and skeptical. "Good consumerism uses more than a dash of skepticism," says Richard Laermer, author of the insightful 2009 book, *Punk Marketing: Get Off Your Ass and Join the Revolution*.

If the Customer Is Always Right, Why Worry?

At about the same time the first malls began opening in the early twentieth century, Chicago retail magnate Marshall Field popularized the cliché "The customer is always right." Many consumers interpreted it to mean they could never be wrong. Talk like that also lulled customers into a false sense of security. After all, if they were always right, then surely they would get what they wanted, right? Buyers had the sense—as more shopping centers sprang up and more businesses parroted a false claim that customers knew what they wanted and when—that even when a business didn't necessarily take care of them that an increasingly activist government, one with an ever-watchful eye, would protect them from predatory companies.

With only a few notable exceptions, the rise of the shuttered proprietary system, and the clever spin of how much they cared about the consumer, thrust the American consumer into a downward spiral of complacency and uncritical thinking. We have yet to recover from it. As for that "activist" government, well, not much good it did us.

Trapped in the System of It All

In a broad sense, walled gardens surround you whenever you set foot outside. But the combination of limited choice and complacency can lead to some of the worst scams I've ever seen. Let me start with a story of my own laziness and a mistake that almost cost me $30,000.

I drive a Honda Accord in a densely populated urban area where I have several choices of dealership. Honda doesn't exactly dole out franchises like candy, but there *is* a choice. However, one particular dealership has gotten our business during the last decade or so because they sold us our last car at a reasonable price and their service department is first rate.

Yet when it comes to sales—that's a different story. We were at the dealership to get new brakes installed one Saturday, and we began wandering around the showroom. It didn't take long for a salesman to materialize, asking us if we wanted to drive the newest

Accord. Our car had just passed its 100,000-mile anniversary, so we agreed.

Within a few minutes, we'd settled on a price for both our old car (mistake #2—never do a trade-in; they make a killing on it) and were prepared to make an offer on a new set of wheels. It was more money than we'd ever spent to drive off the lot. Then the once-friendly salesman zinged us: "We do not negotiate on price."

Negotiation is a time-honored practice among automobile dealers, and it will be one right up to and including the flying car. The sticker price is a known nonentity; it's called "above tissue," which means it is inflated by a ton of money from what the dealer purchased it for ("tissue").

If everyone paid sticker price, the dealership would be rolling in it, and motorists would be suckers. So I was astonished when the salesman told me *everyone* paid sticker and that somehow all his customers were "very" satisfied. I suspected this was an outright lie.

I did what any self-respecting consumer advocate would do: I told him, well, I need some time to think about the price. Both of us knew I was walking away. His manager pursued me in the parking lot to explain why it was so important to pay the full sticker price. None of his reasons made any sense. ("It wouldn't be fair to the others!") I listened and left.

From that day forward I wondered how many customers *didn't* walk away from this scam. Paying sticker price for a car is off-highway robbery. How many people had come to have an auto serviced and while waiting were cajoled into buying something new? How many, like me, would do so without even asking the dealership across town for a competing quote?

The dealership was a kind of walled garden—and that prison wall was high.

If someone who finds scams for a living can get caught in the spiral of complacency, anyone can. In the weeks after the near-debacle, I wondered how I could have failed to do the most basic due diligence. Was I looking for something too easy, like the ability to drive away happy? Had I been conditioned to think that because my dealership provided such terrific service, of course it wouldn't rip me off when it sold me something new? Complacency! Being inside the garden made me think I was safe and secure.

I see people making stupid decisions every day. In some product categories, 80 percent of all purchases are so-called impulse buys that appear to be made at the spur of the moment (they may not be so impulsive, as I'll show you later). Billions a year are spent on these purchases—whether it's sweet candy stacked at eye level or a shiny new car parked near a slickly polished service desk.

Do You Suffer from Walled Garden Syndrome?

I have a name for consumers who behave as if they're shopping in a prison, either real or imagined. These buyers suffer from Walled Garden Syndrome, which I define as consumers who willingly, and often subconsciously, give up choice for the sake of convenience. And you don't necessarily have to make unwise purchasing decisions in order to suffer from WGS. Here are a few questions you might ask yourself to see if you are a victim.

- *Do you just "go shopping" sometimes?* An unplanned visit to a shopping center or an afternoon spent browsing the Internet for fun can lead to a poorly advised impulse buy. You're not an engaged consumer; you're just buying what's in front of you then and there.
- *Do you always go shopping at the same place even when its prices go up?* Walled Garden Syndrome isn't about actual limits in choice, but perceived ones. If you wouldn't dream of shopping with a competitor, you're restricting your own options and may suffer from this syndrome.
- *Do you really compare prices?* Savvy shoppers not afflicted by WGS never roll over for the first offer even if it's marked down from sticker. Instead, they methodically compare prices and user-generated ratings to ensure they have the best deal. Then they wait for the product to go on sale—and then pounce.
- *Is convenience the most important thing to you?* As a guy who doesn't really like shopping, I understand this one best. That's me. When I have to purchase something, I want to be done with it. So if a nearby store carries the product, I'd rather drive over, buy it, and be finished. (I have other family members for whom shopping is a game, and they're immune to this tendency.)

The worst walled gardens aren't the ones built by mall landlords or technology overlords. They're the ones inside your head, raised by your lax attitude toward buying and reinforced with tantalizing advertising of companies benefiting from them. And the first step to breaking free is becoming aware that you're in that prison. I suspect Walled Garden Syndrome is driven by the fear of loss. We've evolved to be unconsciously risk averse and to want to minimize feelings of regret in the future. But by consciously pushing ourselves out of our comfort zone, we can usually achieve more in all aspects of life, not just as consumers.

Walled gardens and closed systems are not an inevitable part of life. When consumers resist them, market pressure gives way to innovation, openness, and greater choice. For example, malls are facing surprisingly robust competition from revived downtowns and other unenclosed shopping districts these days; they're said to be in decline, as consumers look for new places to spend their money. Witness, too, the rise of open-source computer operating system Linux, which chips away at Microsoft's dominant Windows market share year upon year.

Businesses love walled gardens of every kind, because first, its customers pay more, and second, it has to give less. All are good reasons for you to resist the walled gardens in which you find yourself as a consumer.

But there are other ways businesses entice you to become docile and in which you willingly—and even compulsively—participate.

8

The Price of Loyalty

Habit is stronger than reason.

—George Santayana

THE LETTER ALTERNATED between begging and threatening its intended recipient. It was addressed to a vice president at United Airlines from a 25-year-old editor at an influential travel magazine—an editor who had avidly collected frequent flier miles during the prior year in a compulsive effort to reach coveted elite status level.

He knew his ability to become a Premier-Level passenger would ensure extra-special treatment by the airline: upgrades, priority boarding, a separate phone line for reservations, and a somewhat improved flying experience (anything is an improvement). Unfortunately, he was just a few miles short of what he needed. He begged the VP to make this one-time exception and grant him Premier status. But he didn't need to articulate the threat; it was implied by the letterhead and the signature. "Turn me down, and I'll write nasty things about you."

I know about the letter, because I wrote it.

Who wouldn't crave elite status? But while there's a rational explanation for wanting to become either Premier or Premier

Executive (even better)—specifically, that you're treated like you exist—there's no rational explanation for what I would have done to get it. I spent a whole year intentionally steering all travel plans toward United, often taking more expensive, less convenient flights or flights I didn't even need to take. (Yes, it's *that* desperate.)

My name is Chris, and I am a frequent-flier-a-holic. And I'm ashamed of my unethical behavior while trying to finagle elite membership from United. But now, two decades later, I really understand the motives that drove my act of desperation. Yeah, I was young and impulsive—well, young*ish*—but I was also under the control of a seductive program that is both highly addictive and controlling.

Unsurprisingly, United buckled under my threat, even though I had no intention of carrying it out (I say that in the light of day, right?) and granted me Premier status as a "one-time" exception. The airline needs more Premier members like me, I still reason, because it knows they're likely to try even harder to reach the next rung of the elite ladder, spending more money in an effort to attain that elusive Gold, Platinum, or Diamond level. Yet unless you're a travel writer or a member of Congress or have more than 100,000 Twitter followers or can shout louder than my five-year-old, it's unlikely any airline will even *consider* helping you out if you fall short.

Loyalty programs have boomed since I tried to become a VIP at United, expanding to every conceivable business: electronics stores, groceries, e-tailers, casinos, XXX emporiums (no, really, my editor told me about that one), and most of all, anything related to travel. All of these work the same way: You veer your money their way, and they give you a point. The more you spend, the more perks they offer. Around and around we go, like kids on a merry-go-round. Americans accumulate approximately $48 billion in points and miles annually through 2.1 billion loyalty program memberships. It's a national obsession. Research suggests that these loyalty programs are particularly good at swaying customers who would normally shop around for the best deal, the so-called "infrequent players." When they fall under the influence of that loyalty spell, they often change their buying patterns, as I did with the goal of the well-named elite status (also sometimes called *elitism*).

And for what? Consumers fail to redeem at least one-third of the points, essentially throwing away $16 billion. Put differently, the average household that participates in loyalty programs earns $622 worth of miles in a year, but lets $205 of those lapse. That's enough money to buy a cheap airline ticket outright. And, oh yeah, United now offers miles for online purchases made through a special "United browser update" that tracks where and how you spend it.

What Loyalty Programs Make Us Do

To get a better idea of how loyalty programs sway you and me, consider those offered by most major credit card companies.

- *Close to half* of all Visa and MasterCard issuers now operate a rewards program tied to their credit card offering and *nearly a quarter* of debit cards do.
- *More than a quarter* of customers reported that they are "extremely likely" to increase their visits to a business if they have a loyalty reward card for them.
- *More than 60 percent* of U.S. households said that loyalty card programs were important in their shopping decisions.
- Not surprisingly, customer spending is *46 percent higher* with companies that offer reward card programs.

What You Need to Know before You Sign Up

Thinking of registering for a loyalty program? Here are a few things you need to know before you do:

- *Make sure it's the right place for you.* Are you participating in the program because of the generous rewards or because you genuinely like this service or product? If the program is your major reason, then don't walk away—*run*. If you don't like the product, even a fantastic loyalty program won't be enough to keep you happy. Quite the contrary, you will hate yourself in the morning.

(continued)

(*continued*)

- *Do the math.* Pay close attention to the rate at which you can earn value in the program, its earning velocity, and the attractiveness of the rewards. If the numbers don't add up, then forget it. (For example, some loyalty programs offer a "free" companion airline ticket if you sign up for a credit card. But read the fine print: The first ticket must be an over-priced full-fare economy class ticket. You could probably buy two discounted tickets for that price, if not three or four.)

- *Don't let it control you.* Don't spend at levels you can't afford or buy anything you don't need simply to rack up points. And don't, please, fly to Seattle and back in a single day to earn points. (Yeah, I'm talking to *you*.)

- *Make sure the program listens to you.* The most forward-looking loyalty programs are designed to converse *with* customers, not simply bombard you with offers and spam you daily. Look for evidence that the company is paying attention to feedback, both in person and via social media channels, like Facebook, Google+, your own blog, and Twitter.

- *Read the privacy policy.* Are you signing your life away or authorizing the program to send nonstop offers from third parties? If so, this is a sign the company doesn't respect your privacy. Becoming a member could be—here's the pun—pointless.

- *If you're an infrequent customer, just say no.* A lot of businesses will pressure you to become part of their loyalty program on your first purchase by offering a discount, which is like asking for your second date before the first one gets started. Don't join unless you're actually a frequent customer and plan to continue.

- *Remember, loyalty is a one-way street.* Just because it's called loyalty doesn't mean that the company is loyal to *you*. In fact, it normally means they won't reciprocate. They simply want you to be loyal to them so that they make money. I'm sure when American Airlines started the first modern-day loyalty program a generation ago, loyalty was the last thing on their mind, and sadly it's true.

Personally, I'm still not keen on most loyalty programs, even if you dutifully follow these guidelines. If you take a hard look at most of them, you'll realize that they're intended to turn you into a compulsive customer who is blindly loyal to a company and its products. Do you really want to go down that road? Or fly in *their* sky?

In some cases the best offers in loyalty programs are sent to customers who are less loyal and whom the company is trying hard to attract back—more of a disloyalty program. When you join a loyalty program, you make it easy for the company to track all your behavior as their customer. Essentially, you are giving them the information to market to you more effectively. Guess who is likely to benefit from this data?

What Makes Loyalty Programs Dangerous

So what was it that turned me from a card-carrying United Airlines frequent flier into a frequent-flier program skeptic—indeed, skeptical of nearly every program like it that exists? The answer: years of experience covering customer service as a reporter and a human being.

Wanting to become Premier, you see, was just a natural reaction on my part to the horrors of being stuck back there in coach. But take a step back with me, and you'll see a system that's fundamentally wrong.

Whether you're shopping at Safeway (where everything is marked up beyond reason and then "discounted" for Safeway Club loyalists), or staying at a hotel that places their elite-level guests in the choicest rooms while sending bargain-hunting nobodies to the worst quarters (next to the elevator, just below the disco, opposite the ice machine), the programs divide us into distinctive haves and have-nots.

But that's not the worst of it. These divisions often give employees a tacit license to treat members with respect and deference while ignoring basically anybody else's needs. Talk about a dumb way to do business. This two-tiered customer service is terribly misguided. It isn't so much a reward they're offering to the frequent customers as much as a punishment for consumers who have the audacity to shop for the best deal and who dared not enroll where they should have.

I've come to believe there's no such thing as a loyalty win-win. I think there's a steep and often hidden price to be paid when you participate in said programs. The game can easily turn into an obsession that disables your common sense, compelling you to make completely irrational purchasing decisions. And you also find out just what an airline or hotel *really* thinks of you when you come down to "regular" levels.

Pudding Guy

Exhibit A in the obsessive behavior category is David Phillips, a civil engineer at the University of California at Davis, also known as the Pudding Guy. Back in 1999, he took advantage of a mileage promotion on boxes of Healthy Choice Foods to rack up 1,253,000 frequent flier miles. How'd he do that? The promotion had no limits on the number of boxes that could be redeemed, so he hit several grocery stores in Sacramento, buying a total of 12,150 individual servings of pudding for $3,140. In doing so, he acquired the right to about 50 round-trip economy class tickets worth about $12,500, roughly quadrupling his investment. When his story began making the rounds online—and later in newspapers read by frequent travelers—he became an overnight cult hero. What a guy!

I'm not just talking about my own propensity for choosing United flights, even when cheaper and more direct routes were available. I witnessed incidents all around me where people made rash consumer choices for the express purpose of generating more rewards. At about the same time when I was struggling to achieve elite status, my roommate confessed he'd put nearly six figures' worth of computer equipment purchases on his rewards credit card to take advantage of a two-for-one offer on points. He netted more than 200,000 miles. How coincidental that his consulting firm needed the equipment at exactly the same time his card was running the promotion. The mileage collection schemes have only become more sophisticated. The latest, which came to light in 2011, involved a conspiracy to buy dollar coins through the U.S. Mint through a credit card that awarded miles and redeposit them in your bank, paying off your card. Clever? No doubt. Unethical? Probably.

Truth is—and you can mouth these words if you have a rewards card—that the promise of points can override your common sense and trigger you to make a purchasing decision that you otherwise would not make. Ever.

Confessions of an Elite

A few years ago, a large hotel chain approached me about doing some consulting work. Instead of paying me the going rate, it offered me less money along with what's called in kind—a fancy way of saying it would compensate for its ridiculous cheapness by giving me products worth money. Kind of like living a game show. How about a lifetime frequent-guest membership with half a million points? Instead of sticking to my standard rate of being paid so I can feed my family, I reluctantly said sure. It might be nice to find out how the other half lives, I reasoned. Until then, I had steadfastly refused to play the loyalty game as a way of life. And now I know why.

When I checked into one of the chain's properties, I suddenly felt like a million bucks. Rooms were quietly upgraded from standard (half a room) to deluxe (a full room) to junior suite (a full room and an alcove) to a lovely suite. Housed in the latter, I learned that bottled water and Internet connections were complimentary. Gifts awaited me in my room—fruit galore! When I pushed "0" to talk with an operator, it was always answered on the first ring, with a cheerful, "How may I help you, Mr. Elliott?"

I was embarrassed and disappointed by the oddness of it all— embarrassed by how obsequious the hotel staff acted toward a super-elite guest (even if I really wasn't one) and disappointed to compare my treatment with the mediocre service grudgingly

(continued)

(*continued*)
offered to the poor slobs of whom I had been one before today. As long as I flashed my card—and flash is the operative word—no request was too big. Now I know why guests often trade their time and energy for elite status. I mean, the water was *free*.

I might be more understanding of loyalty programs if they could be a bit more consistent in their dealings with their members—but they're slippery. Consider the maddening terms and conditions that stipulate how points and miles don't belong to you but that the airlines own them outright. Or that these mamas can change the rules anytime without notice. (See what American Airlines' terms and conditions say: "Accrued mileage credit and award tickets do not constitute property of the member. American Airlines may, in its discretion, change the AAdvantage program rules, regulations, travel awards and special offers at any time with or without notice.")

The rewards are not real. The programs are scams. And the winners in this loyalty game are the companies that have seduced their seemingly best customers with creature comforts and perks that, in a world I want to live in, everyone should get. The losers are all of us. Not just the regular buyers who refuse to buy into this nonsense but also the elite lemmings who have blind brand loyalty even to a giant chain like Hilton Hotels, which has gone from a traveler's dream choice to a cheap cog in the BlackRock portfolio.

How to Save Money

The worst loyalty programs are the ones you have to pay for *and* that take your valuable business. Those include affinity credit cards that charge a high annual fee for the privilege of earning miles or points, or cinema loyalty programs that cost money *and* demand your loyalty. I was at the movies last weekend when a woman selling tickets asked me, with a completely straight face, if I wanted to pay $12 to belong to her theater chain's frequent-customer program. My response? "I think you should be paying *me*." Don't be tempted by these offers. They're as wrong and unnecessary as an "extended" warranty.

The Loyalty Effect

Trying to determine what effect loyalty programs have had on one or two consumers is easy. But figuring out what they've done to overall consumer behavior is trickier. Loyalty programs of one sort or another have been an integral part of our economy since almost the beginning of commerce, when the caveman selling clubs gave his best customer a break on the late model dino-slayer. (It was—wait for it—the first loyalty "club.") But modern-day loyalty programs—with their cards and points and perks and turned-up noses—only go back a few decades to the middle of last century. The most visible of these are the travel-related programs, such as airline and hotel programs— and the first contemporary loyalty scheme was American Airlines' AAdvantage program, which took off in early 1981.

We know that loyalty can boost business for a single company. For example, casino biggie Harrah's in 2005 started a then-unique program titled Total Rewards. The program would track how often guests pulled the lever of a one-armed bandit, how much one bet at the table, and even personal inclinations such as what time of year you like to visit, where you eat, what kind of accommodations you ask for, and how much you fluff your pillow (kidding). It's credited with boosting spending by loyal gamblers anywhere from 36 percent to 45 percent, which at the time was considered unreal and outrageous and something other companies would drool over. Today Total Rewards is totally old news, and much of corporate America has imitated what Harrah's did while reaping similar returns in the loyalty game.

The $48 billion points that consumers collect every year represent only a small portion of loyalty programs' overall value. Remember, that's just the value of the points; there's usually a purchase attached to it, too. When you look at it that way, it's not hard to conclude that loyalty schemes influence a formidable chunk of commerce in the United States. Conservatively, you could term this the loyalty effect, although more cynical observers might also correctly refer to it as a loyalty economy.

You're Complicit

Every time you make a purchase in order to enhance your status or acquire rewards, you are fueling this loyalty economy with your hard-earned dollars without knowing it. You may be in denial, arguing you'd have to buy this stuff anyway. And most members would deny with arms folded that any such programs are controlling them. But take it from someone who has been a happy victim of a program and ultimately witnessed its corrosive side effects, I have found that loyalty programs could be one of the greatest creative scams perpetrated on the public. These special-member-only, vaporous set-ups lavish perks on the chosen who have climbed a quixotic ladder; they relegate those who refuse to be sucked in to lousy service and, worse, higher prices; and thanks to these systems, consumers waste billions playing the game.

I'm not going to single-handedly eliminate loyalty programs. My mission, and I accept it, is to raise consumers' awareness to avoid their snares. The trick is to become mindful of loyalty programs' influence at the point of sale. Ask yourself: *At the moment I choose a product, is someone else steering my hard-to-hold dollars to a place that promises reward without my caring about* anything *but the reward?* (Picture a dog panting at a bone but only if he is a "good boy.") The easiest way to end it is to cut your loyalty card up right now, cancel your membership, and decide what to buy based on price and quality; rewards be damned!

Reality check: If you travel or shop with one company almost all the time, it would be madness *not* to collect points, so in that case please leave the scissors in its sheath. Here you have to weigh decisions with your conscience and avoid the loyalty trap with your own good sense. Keep in mind that you're playing with danger if you ask the hard questions above and find you've been handing out money to the wrong guys all along.

Why aren't more consumer advocates and helping-hand journalists warning us about the damage a loyalty program can inflict? Why, you have to wonder, do many "experts" advise their audiences to freely participate in these and other scams?

One, because those companies are constantly reminding them of how great they are to customers. And sometimes hyperbole goes a long way. And two, I say with a grin, because they are not only covering these clubs for men and women, but they are members, too.

Questions to Ask before You Buy

If you belong to a loyalty program, here are some questions you'd ask before whipping out the debit card.

- *Do I need what I'm buying?* In truth, this is a good question to ask whether you're a member of a program or not, no matter what's in your hand.
- *Will this purchase do more for me or for my rewards?* Buying something just because it enhances your rewards is classically destructive—and fairly pointless—purchasing behavior.
- Is this what I'd consider "rational behavior"? This of course begins with the assumption you are rational at heart; if not, skip down. But everyone else: If you're factoring price, quality, and convenience into your decision, there's nothing to worry about yet; if it's all about the points, then you might want to think again. And again.
- *What would my actions be if I hadn't joined this club?* If you really need (read: not desire) this product, if it's necessary, if you're behaving like a normal functioning societal human, then there's always one more question: Would you still buy it if you weren't a member? If you'd still buy it no matter what club would have you as a member, then go for it.

9

When the Watchdogs Sleep

Let sleeping dogs lie.

—Olde American proverb

I KNOW WHAT it's like to be a sleeping watchdog because I am occasionally turned into one. Distracting a consumer journalist is easy. During my tenure as a financial reporter, a publicist for a prominent Wall Street company—an affable guy who always returned my calls quickly—offered me tickets to a hockey game one afternoon.

I'm no hockey fan, and my company had a no-gifting policy, so I declined. But just the offer was enough for me to soften my coverage of his organization. I was so changed by this gesture of friendship in a city where I knew no one—often feeling pretty lonely when I left work—that I'd skim over negative stories that popped up about his firm.

Liking Hockey Guy turned out to be a mistake—and a serious one at that. Many years later, long after I'd moved on, the company was revealed to be a key player in the 2008 financial meltdown.

So, if the promise of seats at an NHL game could persuade someone *with* a functional moral compass to go easy on a Wall Street corporation, then what other perks might be tempting watchdogs such as me to turn a blind eye? In my two decades as a journalist, I've seen so many self-described champions of consumer rights let their guards down with the shrug of a shoulder that it's embarrassing to count them. (It's especially upsetting when I acknowledge it; let's just say I'm atoning now.) Not only do my fellow consumer advocates willfully disregard news they should cover with a vengeance; the worst part is that many of the most influential voices in consumer journalism have shaken off their watchdog collars in recent years because there is just no money in it.

Which brings up another consideration: While the pressure from publicity folks and advertisers is considerable, it pales when compared side by side with the power a reader exerts on the trained eyes keeping an eye on those corporations who could be doing evil. When consumers prefer one kind of story or publication over another, the results are stunning. Add in how the watchdogs are compensated, and you have a heated recipe for trouble.

How Much, If Anything, Would You Be Willing to Pay per Month in Order to Read a Daily Newspaper Online?	
Possible Price	*Number Willing to Pay*
More than $20	1 percent
$11–$20	4 percent
$1–$10	19 percent
Nothing	77 percent

Source: Adweek/Harris.

In the age of "information wants to be free," few people are willing to pay for a subscription to a daily newspaper (although many seem okay with community weeklies because that's where all the good coupons are). You would assume that so-called educated people would understand the value of accountable news, yet 72 percent of college grads claim they'd pay zero to read a newspaper today. Most disturbing is how older readers (the smart, mature 55+) who at one time were a paper's core audience, are now least likely to pay for news. More than 80 percent of seniors say they wouldn't shell out a penny for access to the press.

Given the diminished financial value that readers see in real news, it's easy to conclude that they'd care little about how the product is created. However, no. In an age where a story's success is based on the number of click-throughs and comments, the one imbibing the story has the power.

So what do readers want to see, read, or hear? Here are the five most popular stories of 2010 on the ABC News show *Good Morning America*, as determined by an analysis of site visitation:

1. "Michael Jackson's Former Bodyguards Talk about Jackson's Secret Life"
2. "Joran Confesses to Peruvian Murder"
3. "Elin Nordegren Opens Up About Tiger Woods' Affairs and Their Divorce"
4. "Attorney General's Blunt Warning on Terror Attacks"
5. "Inside Lindsay Lohan's Medicine Cabinet"

The only hard news story is number 4, the one about Eric Holder's terror warnings—and that has nothing to do with the victimization of ordinary Americans by deep-pocketed corporations and other scammers. There are no exposés on the entire list of favorite stories about product recalls, scams, or consumer warnings (although you'll find a ton of stories about the latest season of ABC's own *Dancing with the Stars* and a report about Shamu killing his trainer at SeaWorld farther down the list).

So now you see that since people say they aren't willing to pay for hard news, they really are saying they prefer articles or posts or anchored pieces or even tweets about Michael Jackson's bodyguards and Tiger Woods' divorce, rather than news on who's ripping them off. Follow the numbers, and it makes consumer journalism a difficult sell to those paying the bills. Add that to endless hours of deep digging to come up with an airtight exposé of wrongdoing, and now we find it might be only glanced at by a tiny number of readers. So here is the result: a decimated and underpaid (if paid at all) corps of consumer advocates who are tempted every day to toss in the towel.

And now you may play a tiny violin for me.

Where Have the Watchdogs Gone?

Although there are bright spots such as nonprofit online news organization ProPublica, the research group Pew Foundation, and Consumers Union, publishers of *Consumer Reports* magazine (reader-supported by more than four million subscribers), the landscape for consumer news is pretty bleak. There are some watchdogs toiling hard to protect consumers' rights (many I know personally); it is a story of the ages to explain what the heck happened to the biggest names in consumer journalism.

Take those Stosselesque–celebrated TV talking heads who made a name in the hypercompetitive Los Angeles TV market. The one best known is David Horowitz, whom I idolized while in college out west. In the years since he left TV, this once-feared consumer gadfly has made a living touting causes for pay. Horowitz is said to have received $106,000 in 1998 to speak out against a state ballot measure to slash electricity rates. Years later, Horowitz received an unknown sum to fight a Los Angeles City Council proposal to force cable TV companies to open high-speed lines to competitors. Although Horowitz still stands up for consumer rights, he now charges $50 for an over-the-phone consultation and $250 to do a bit of legwork on anyone's behalf. I wouldn't call that journalism, but that's just me.

Another consumer advocate, Alan Mendelson, was a capable biz and personal finance reporter for TV station KCAL, having spent years steering viewers to the best buys in the Southland. But he lost his job in 2006 and now he produces infomercials. Yet another LA consumer reporter—Judd McIlvain of KTTV and KCBS—well known for his aggressive troubleshooter reporting—was laid off more than a decade ago and produces ads for car and home loan companies.

And what about John Stossel? He's on FOX News, doing his bosses' bidding for big bucks.

Who Do You Trust?

I consulted with—or tried to consult with—every nationally known consumer advocate for this project. Some of them replied immediately and were generous with their time, offering helpful insights and feedback (see the Acknowledgments). Others ignored me, even after numerous attempts to contact them. I'm grateful for both responses, actually. It gave me a clearer picture of which consumer journalists working today are here to truly help people (because what self-respecting consumer advocate can turn down a request for help?) and which ones have no interest in promoting anyone but themselves. No, I won't name names. But I've recommended the ones that I think are doing an outstanding job in this book and on my site, On Your Side (www.onyoursi.de).

It's difficult to find fault with them for wanting to feed their families. Some of them got laid off at their peak by short-sighted management. Consumer journalism is not cheap, I'll admit, not just because it demands an experienced reporter with better-than-average instincts but because said investigations can drag on for months. And if someone is looking into big corporations, an advocate's employer stands to lose huge amounts of advertising revenue.

Yes, there is still good consumer reporting being conducted these days. *Consumer Reports'* coverage of fraudulent extended warranties, that earn companies more money than any product, comes to mind. And so does ProPublica's thorough reporting on Wall Street misdeeds that scored it a Pulitzer Prize. But what *isn't* being investigated, now that consumer journalism, with its irresistible gotcha stories, has been reduced to five minutes at the end of the 11 o'clock local newscast? And what *isn't* being covered, now that many large papers have either laid off their consumer reporters or the topic only merits a short quarter-page column on Saturday, a day hardly anyone reads news?

I have a good idea, based on complaints I get nearly every day, that for every investigative story that could shed light on a company's wrongdoing, or worse, there are probably a hundred similarly legit problems that just get glossed over. And if I had a dollar coin for every time I've seen an e-mail that started, "You're probably too busy to answer me," I'd be writing this from the upstairs study of my very own McMansion. Companies are getting away with murder—and I mean that figuratively, but who knows these days?—since the watch hounds are all but extinct. And when the dogs leave the yard, the wolves come out to dine on the flock.

When Dogs Follow the Wrong Scent . . .

Another unfortunate truth is that consumer reporters who remain on the job get it wrong and mislead readers, viewers, and clickers who rely on them for the goods. How do I know? Because I've *been* one of those reporters—sure, I'm big enough to admit I've gotten it wrong on numerous occasions. Errors are inevitable when you're a consumer reporter, and for everyone in every line, but in the case of pro journalists, even the best slip up. But there's a wide chasm between errors and outright misrepresentations. For example, weekly newsmagazine *Dateline NBC* aired a segment in 1992 that purported to show GM trucks blowing up each time these bad boys crashed. Turned out the show's producers attached toy rockets to ensure an explosion and the incident became a huge scandal and led to the resignation of NBC News president Michael Gartner.

In recent years *Consumer Reports* has come under fire for some of its coverage. Just a few years before NBC's GM fiasco, *Consumer Reports* declared Suzuki's Samurai "not acceptable" because of its propensity for tipping over in road tests. Suzuki sued and claimed the *Consumer Reports* test was designed to make the SUV tip over. The two parties settled after a protracted battle.

And *then* CR found itself in hot water in 2007, this time over crash tests of infant car seats by warning that only 2 of 12 seats it tested were worth buying. However, instead of conducting the tests at 38 miles an hour as they claimed, they were done at 70 mph. Oops. *Consumer Reports* issued an embarrassing retraction.

Ironically, I had pitched *Consumer Reports* with a story about bogus ratings systems at about the same time, though my ratings investigation had nothing to do with car seats. The nonprofit's organization's lawyers and fact-checkers were all over my text almost immediately, obsessively trying to disprove what I had written.

Needless to say, that's no way to advocate for consumers. Sadly, my story—which was 100 percent proven accurate and would have helped millions of readers—was pulled after the lawyers made mincemeat of it. But I can understand their caution; they didn't want another car seat fiasco on their hands.

Why do the watchdogs go down the wrong path? Here are a few reasons:

- *Lack of resources.* A single consumer reporter—even the greatest—can be easily misled or get sidetracked pursuing a story. Without a team of researchers and a wise, level-headed editor or producer, mistakes happen—and happen more frequently.
- *An us vs. them mentality.* Journalists who go after corporate entities for misdeeds often see the world in black and white. The readers are *victims*; the company is *the bad guy.* If you have a gut feeling and a bit of evidence that someone is up to no good, you could be right . . . or you could be wrong.
- *Lack of support.* Cutting back the consumer reporter to a part-time position or eliminating it entirely sends a message that you don't care about consumer issues—or consumers. When media organizations pay little or nothing for the coverage, they get little from it. Or nothing.
- *Wanting it to be true—even when it isn't.* Everyone loves a good dramatic tale, whether it's about a faulty car seat or an exploding truck. It's simple human nature to push the envelope, to make something that looks true seem a little bolder than it really is. Add a lack of support, resources, and an inherent distrust of corporate America, and you can end up with something that's pretty darn false—but a "good" story!

In a world where consumer reporters are rewarded for churning out stories with stop-the-press headlines that tend to get splattered across the likes of the *Huffington Post* and *Drudge Report*, is it any wonder that sloppy reporting happens? I'd like to see the downward spiral of sensationalist advocacy stories stopped. And with the risk of sounding like Sally Struthers, *you* can help save consumer journalism.

How to Tell If a Story Is Wrong-Headed

There's no surefire way to determine at face value if the story you're reading is true or false. Just as purchasing decisions are often controlled by subconscious emotions that we are not aware of, so too is your sense of right and wrong. Consider some questions when you see these tales of Warning!

Does it look unbelievable? Exploding trucks, SUVs tipping over, unsafe infant seats: the idea of these happening *en masse* lacks credibility. When was the last time you heard of a truck exploding, except maybe in a Michael Bay flick?

Does the company heatedly deny the allegations in a nonstop campaign? That doesn't necessarily mean the tales are tall, but when the company holds a press conference to denounce the story, as GM did, or sues the media outlet, as in Suzuki v. Consumers Union, then I'd bet the corporate side hasn't been fully explored.

Is the blogosphere denouncing the story? When social media trounces a report—when the mob goes after it—it's safe to say the original report could be flawed.

Does the tale contradict your own experience? If these new revelations about something unsafe or fraudulent differ from real life, *and* the company vehemently denies what's being said, *and* the social media-ites are sneering toward the reporter in question, it's probably untrue.

Being a Discerning—and Demanding—Consumer

One of the first ways to correct the problem of bad customer service is to insist on having better consumer journalism. As I have noted, keeping effective watchdogs costs money. In 2010, ProPublica, an independent nonprofit organization dedicated to investigative journalism, brought in $9.8 million. The bulk of its income came from contributions, gifts, grants, and quarters found in couches. I've been running a consumer advocacy blog for years, and it also survives— sometimes barely—on donations from readers and some corporate support. I can attest to the fact that good consumer reporting isn't free.

Demanding a pack of first-rate watchdogs means reading, watching, and interacting with the coverage you need. And if you care, *really* care, then fund what you believe in. Supporting programs like public television's investigative program *PBS Frontline* or donating to the Consumerist, an irreverent advocacy blog owned by Consumers Union, will strengthen the ranks of the reporters who are looking out for you.

You must also be discerning in what you take in. Remember, every click and every download is a vote—so when you go nuts staring at the cute kitten all over the video sites (and success is based on *how long* someone stays on a link), then that's a clear message you want more adorable kittens and fewer of the stories that mean anything. Last hint for now: Whenever you skip the important investigation into toy safety or the exposé on a scammer, you send an equally clear message that you don't care about critical learning.

I've had a lot of time to ponder the question of "What matters?" What constitutes the kind of journalism or blogging that is worth encouraging? I say if it makes you a more informed consumer, it's worth it. As always, splashy, award-winning consumer journalism (see Stossel) will get heralded for its guts—because there's a PR machine behind you. But I think we require an equal amount of simple how-to stories you read in magazines, newspapers, and see in blogs or podcasts that enrich our lives as consumers. They can add to our collective consumer IQ incrementally.

I don't expect anyone to stop staring at falling babies and dogs that know the alphabet. But just like in real life, where a daily regimen of cream puffs and soda will kill you faster than Morgan Spurlock's diet, a constant intake of fluffy, crowd-pleasing, pandering "stories" will, like *Three's Company* reruns all day long, turn your brain to mush. Nothing that you learn from Tiger Woods' messy divorce settlement or Lindsay Lohan's medicine chest will make you a better consumer—or person, for that matter. The few and far between watchdogs (who also know the alphabet) now for the most part play for the corporate team. The ones that remain, ahem, are far from perfection. Like PBS before me, I ask that you support and consume the quality.

When you tell the *Huffington Post* or ABCNews.com that you want more intelligent stories, you unlock better customer service from the media conglomerations—and their advertisers. And let's not be naïve here: You may do what is required of you but a collective apathy to fix the broken relationship between companies and customers needs to dim for anything real to happen.

10

Tired, Confused, and Apathetic

There is nothing harder than the softness of indifference.
—Juan Montalvo

IF YOU SPEND just a little time watching shoppers, you'll notice something that many American businesses already know: Most think little about their purchasing decisions. They're much more likely to snatch what catches their eye off the shelves and take it to the checkout counter without contemplation. And if the checkout line is too big, they might just walk out—even if it's a necessity.

I watched this sorry routine repeatedly one recent afternoon on the second floor of a Macy's. Although a few customers appeared to take their time and carefully consider each option, most didn't. For example, I observed one woman in the children's clothing section who was picking out a dress for her daughter. Her choice was obviously an impulse buy, with price and quality taking a backseat to color, style, and her daughter's wishes ("I want a princess dress!"). I asked Mom whether she had done any comparison-shopping. She hadn't.

Disclosure: This little girl happened to also be my daughter. But could I do any better than her mother? Could I tell my own four-year-old that she couldn't have the pink dress because it was overpriced? No way. I studied the behavior of other parents going through the same ritual, who almost all buckled quickly to the whims of their offspring, price be damned. They all seemed to be in a hurry, too.

Research suggests that my observations are far from random. The average purchaser spends just 11 minutes and 27 seconds in the store from start to finish. Additionally, a 2004 study says that children paired with an adult boost the probability of an impulse buy by 18 percent. But those numbers only point to a more profound reality about shopping: We take the path of least resistance. The logic is maddeningly self-destructive. We've worked hard to make our money; why should we have to work hard to spend it?

Truth is, we're so sapped by the come-ons from the Internet, TV, and radio in our always-on world that our powers of resistance have been short-circuited. Window displays are optimized so that they draw our attention from 25 feet away, which extends the amount of time we're being exposed to sales pitches. We're confused, too, because the avalanche of pitches to buy stuff we don't need has overwhelmed our natural aversion to raw deals. Does it really matter, we ask ourselves, if we pay a bit too much for a purchase we don't really want?

I see evidence of consumers' collective despair every day, as folks make questionable purchases and then behave, oh well, as if they had no choice in the matter. It is as if they know they are pawns in a game large companies are playing with multimillion-dollar ad spending, product placement, and massive Internet campaigns; whatever they lose is a foregone conclusion. But these customers are giving themselves to corporate America, who as a group has their way with them, and the future is predetermined. The worst is yet to come.

This apathy trap threatens us all, and it will cost us dearly. No one knows the price tag of failing to do customer due diligence or of allowing savvy marketers to manipulate our families when we go shopping. But it is a higher price than *any* of the frauds or superscams perpetrated on *any* group of consumers by *any* unscrupulous business.

The inevitability of a purchase is among the central theses of Philip Graves' insightful 2010 book *Consumer.ology: The Market Research Myth, the Truth about Consumers and the Psychology of Shopping*. He correctly notes that market research can't accurately predict how you'll act when you're at the store, and that in many ways this is the big mystery of sales. Aha, though; clever companies have found a way to steer "inevitable purchases" their way using everything from lighting techniques to smell (yes, scents are big science!). The inevitable conclusion is that we are only marginally rational animals who can be manipulated. Feeling as if we aren't in control is just one step away from not caring, from feeling like a hamster running around and around.

Are You Stuck in the Apathy Trap?

Here are a few signs that indicate that you might not care.

- *Do you plan your purchases ahead or just wing it when you're in the store?* Customers who visit a store with a specific purchase in mind—and have done some research—are far less likely to be duped into buying.
- *Do you shop because you need to or because you want to?* Buying frivolous items *that you have absolutely no need for* is a gateway drug to being scammed. If you can't tell the difference between these two, you may already be trapped. (If you buy two of an item that's half price, you just neutered the bargain.)
- *Do you enjoy window-shopping or window-browsing?* Spending time in front of the computer mindlessly perusing merchandise or standing in front of a store window opens you to possible manipulation. My advice? *Never* memorize your credit card number—that act makes it too easy to merely hit the link and fill.
- *Do you ask sales associates questions, or do you feel that's bothering them?* To kick the tires is to make a smart purchase. If you'd rather not inconvenience the sales floor staff—who would be out of a job (or bored) if you did not—are you doing any due diligence?
- *Do you care if someone else paid less?* If it doesn't matter to you that another human paid less than you did for a product or

(continued)

> (*continued*)
>
> service, this leads to a slippery slope down to apathy. You should at least ask a friend with first-aid training to check your pulse.
> - *Do you think about what else you might spend on besides the item in your hand/online cart?* Considering what economists call the opportunity cost of a purchase is a good way to erase the gimme-now desire that retailers work hard to instill in you.

These are only a few symptoms of the big problem known as customer apathy. American businesses benefit from the apathy trap because if we don't care, the businesses will happily take our money and we'll accept whatever they offer in return. Even a shoddy product.

If you care enough, or care at all, the chances of this happening to you lessen. The antidote to apathy is just start to care.

Rewiring consumer behavior is easier said than accomplished. Few people *want* more work to do before they shop; that is what research is. To many, shopping is pleasurable time off. Window shopping will surely one day be an Olympic sport.

You can curb your tendency to shop impulsively by taking a wingman or -woman with you who can pull you back before you go whole hog. (This has to be someone you respect and who has your best interests at heart, not a friend who lives vicariously through you.) Be sure to set a budget limit before you leave. Nothing gets me riled up more than spending time on an online forum where someone boasts about how they paid half of what I did for the same product. And here's a hint: use a barcode-scanning app, available for most smartphones, that helps you find the lowest price.

Eyes Wide Shut

In 1997, *Direct Marketing News* estimated each of us sees more ads in one year than people of 50 years ago saw in their lifetime. I could argue that we see more ads in one year than people in 1997 would have in a lifetime. I won't. Let's just say we're exposed to more than 3,000 commercial messages a day through TV, radio, social media, and billboards. You can't turn advertising off; it's always there. Have you been inside a hotel lobby bathroom lately? Everywhere.

Although I don't doubt that marketing that hits us as we walk (or run) affects our purchasing decisions, there are unintended consequences of so much advertising. Having so many messages coming your way is like a tennis machine that goes haywire and hammers you repeatedly. There's no defense. Since you can't get out of the way, you wince as you endure a barrage of speedballs.

I'm baffled how customers have become both so desensitized to messages while simultaneously resigned to falling for them daily, if not hourly. (I promise not to say every second.) Yet that is the perfect description of most spurned consumers who come to me. They know what happened to them. They know it's wrong. They felt powerless to stop it.

Since I began advocating for readers way back in the 1990s, I've noticed a deepening sense of inevitability among readers, as if this assault is unstoppable. And I try to fight this feeling. If the advertising messages were not effective, wouldn't the companies pull the plug? Well, yes. For example, advertisers know that their audiences have shifted from ye olde print to the Internet for their content. According to the Interactive Advertising Bureau (IAB), online advertising revenue in the United States jumped 15 percent in 2010 to a record $26 billion, fully outpacing newspapers, which earned $22.8 billion. Print ad buys have been in decline for more than a decade, and one of the major reasons is because, now that the Net has proven effective to track, it's almost impossible to determine if newspaper ads are worth anything.

For instance, how many people saw an ad and then responded to it? You might be able to make an informed guess on how many folks clipped a coupon, but you'll never know how many readers saw the ad and did anything. Yet web advertising has *analytics* for everything; you can measure effectiveness down to the millisecond.

At the same time, e-mail spam is growing like the worst of weeds, and whether you want to believe it, for the sender, spam *works*. A recent study found 43 percent of users click unsolicited e-mail messages. Sadly, many are still waiting for the wire transfer from Nigeria.

E-Mail Spam

Spam—or unsolicited e-mail—is nothing if not annoying. But it's growing, despite advances in technology.

Year	E-Mails Sent	Percent Spam
2008	76 trillion	70
2009	90 trillion	81
2010	107 trillion	89

Source: Royal Pingdom.

Companies hammer away at us because they eventually get what they want—money—as we respond like sheep to the ads and other marketing detritus. When we stop buying, they call the item "new and improved" or mix the media or change the message or hire Kathy Ireland, but they continue to knock at our heads because it drives cash register movement. What the corporations did not anticipate, which is what I see daily, is how overloaded we've become by messages, period. The net effect is the rise of the zombie customer who, like Freddy Krueger before us, responds more by instinct than intellect, and moves away from the fire and sunlight, or whatever Frankenstein's Monster was afraid of. The zombie consumer can't make rational decisions. The consumer who just does what he is told is there to be controlled. Technology makes it easier to bombard each of us. If response rates drop, no problem. They'll just find another way to getcha.

Decisions, Decisions

Is it any wonder that consumers are so confused? On one hand we've accepted the inevitability of our purchase and the bad service that often comes with it. Yet we seem at times incapable of making a decision that's right for us. That's because we the customer are not merely battered by incessant advertising, we are also maddened by the crush of choices given us. A mere 12 TV channels 20 years ago has multiplied into more than a thousand. Starbucks offers a multitude of possible drink combinations—more than 100,000. Crest has so many distinctive styles of toothpaste that no single drugstore could possibly carry them all.

Researchers have found that when you go to the grocery store and see hundreds of cereals, you are suddenly afflicted by what is called decision fatigue and eventually, choice paralysis. Three things tend to happen: You can default to the tried-and-true, reach for the Corn Flakes or Cheerios. You can try something new, like the new dried blueberry and flaxseed cereal. Or you can do nothing. Sometimes doing nothing is far easier. You go home and eat toast.

We are creatures of habit, so defaulting to a comfortable choice is understandable. But that also helps one company become dominant and lazy—a business that then fails to innovate therefore fails to serve its customers. Those of us brave enough to resist will eventually get beaten down by the nonstop ads, and those of us who aren't able to resist them are doomed to give the incumbents our business again. And again.

How to Save Money

Be the person who knows what you want *before* getting to the store. This will help you narrow choices, thereby eliminating a whole hill of confusion. If you're facing a choice between Count Chocula, Cheerios, and Rice Krispies, you don't have to inspect all the brands and all old and new incarnations that make up an entire aisle—just the prices on the boxes and anything that's been discounted—in order to make a sensible decision.

This drives advertisers crazy, because their pitches don't stand a chance.

When You Don't Make a Decision . . .

Businesses adore the confusion and delight in our standing agog at the rows of cereal boxes. It means that we are open to suggestions, even something as blatantly disgusting as Banana Chocolate Cheerios. (Why would anyone ruin chocolate and bananas, two of the main reasons for living?) Me, I spent a lot of time standing in the cereal aisle of my local grocer's watching as people browsed. Some, if not most, did not look pleased; either they were indecisive, or they were having trouble finding the cereal they wanted. They never looked like they wanted to be there.

Quite a few of them finally made a decision, if that's what it really was, when they reached down and pulled a coupon out of a handy dispenser offering them 50 cents off a box of cereal they'd probably never tried—indeed, one they would likely regret. (I fell for that ruse twice, no less, and was forced *both times* to throw down the entire contents of what I am sure was woodchips or cardboard; no one in my family would go near it. Not even the cats.)

A coupon machine can lift sales of a product by between 18 and 34 percent. The lesson? If you don't make a decision, someone— probably the product's manufacturer—will make one for you.

Dereliction of Duty

From my perspective as a consumer advocate, this rampant customer confusion and fatigue has led to the dereliction of duty— yours. Many have just stopped caring about the basics of being a good customer. So Uncle Chris will now hand you the basics. A good customer is:

- *Informed.* Ideal customers have nothing but the facts on their side. Each of these people-on-a-mission is aware of how much an item costs, has read the warranty, and knows what others are raving or criticizing about it before purchasing the thing.
- *Enlightened.* Understanding the system is key to avoid being victimized by it. Businesses aren't charities—they are well-run profit machines (think Mr. Burns). For the record, there's nothing wrong with that; it is the corporation's main purpose, besides denying overtime, and it is what drives our economy, like it or not. It is your job to do some homework on whether the profit said company makes is deserved.
- *Frugal.* Money doesn't grow on trees, at least not yet. But the very best customers keep a close watch on everything they earn. That money is hard to come by! These beautiful people run the

numbers before they purchase and have a pretty good idea of what they will spend before they reach the checkout. Read that again: before the checkout.

■ *Polite.* As counterintuitive as it might sound, politeness is your most powerful weapon when dealing with any company. Smart customers know they mustn't wait until there's a problem to exhibit that exemplary trait—they always deploy it. Politeness has a magical effect on service providers: they treat you with respect and sometimes even bend over backward to satisfy you. Wouldn't you be more inclined to side with a customer who treated you with respect than one who acted as though you were a crook? (Also note: In person, a salesperson who is treated like an equal, which is quite a rarity, will take the time to steer you to the better deal—even alerting you when it occurs in the near future.)

■ *Resourceful.* That smart customer has learned there's strength in numbers and can find the info he needs to help his cause both online and off. He visits forums and blogs, trades tips, and clips coupons.

■ *Persistent.* A fine upstanding consumer knows that sometimes even the best companies need a nudge or two to do the right thing. He isn't afraid to ask; he feels it's his right—nay, *duty.* Nor does this wonderful being feel he is imposing when asking a sales associate for help at all.

(See "Polite," above.)

■ *Right.* Contrary to what everyone has said since the Renaissance, the customer is *not* always right. The customer *is* correct almost all the time when he has done the research and has the background on his side. Of course, customers can be wrong, too. For instance, the price tag may have turned out wrong. That happens.

When customers give up, they're not just confused and tired; they're abandoning the notion of being good consumers. And when you don't care anymore, then you hand companies the upper hand. They can name their prices, set their terms, offer as little or as much customer service as they feel like—the first time I heard Dell was charging $.99 per minute for its own customers to get tech help I fell off a chair—and we are the lemmings who return again. It is total capitulation—unconditional surrender of the consumer to the corporation. Are you mad yet?

I wish I were exaggerating. Every day, I field calls, e-mails, IMs, texts, and carrier pigeon messages from customers who failed to do even the most basic due diligence—like looking at the final price before clicking the BUY button on an e-commerce site, or reading the terms of their purchase, or asking the most basic questions of the company. They could have easily avoided these problems had they taken consumer responsibility seriously. In most cases, they don't even acknowledge their rights exist. It sucks.

Splitting the Difference

I began by revealing a bunch of troubling new ways that companies try to separate you from your money. From manipulating a corporate image, to tricking search engines, to clever promotions, to marketing that should be illegal, to people posing as customers, companies have perpetrated a scam that affects every customer and will bite you in the derriere before you even know it. Even the most enlightened consumer gets nipped.

Yet I've also described how customers have been complicit because of an unwillingness—and maybe an unawareness—to fulfill an obligation as responsible consumers. Their appetite for actionable knowledge about products is weak. They're fatigued by advertising messages, PR spin, gimmicks galore, and the paradox of consumer choice fatigue. In short, they are beaten down by a well-oiled machine.

I blame everyone. Yes, companies are constantly developing new ways to get inside our high-end wallets, but as I have said, we *let* them in. With a heavy sigh, I report that the bond between consumers and customers, while ostensibly fixable, is fundamentally broken.

And now for something completely different.

How to Fix It

11

The Enlightened Consumer

The world is not a problem; the problem is your unawareness.
—Bunty Bhagwan Shree Rajneesh

ALMOST EVERY CONSUMER complaint is punctuated by one excuse or another. And sometimes several.

The most common? *"Well, gee, Chris, how was I supposed to know?"*

"It's not every single day I buy a new car," one enraged customer wrote, more than a little upset that he took home the biggest lemon on the lot.

And another, after spending twice what she expected for a hotel room: "I'm just not an experienced traveler."

Finally, the one that makes me laugh out loud because in this decade it is hardly true: "I don't know a lot about technology. I'm a Luddite." (A Luddite? Really? Probably more like a technophobe, since there haven't been any real Luddites for at least a century.)

True, you can't be an expert at everything. In the first two sections I told you how companies take advantage, or are smart about getting you to buy, depending on whose viewpoint you see it from. I disclosed the ways we the consumer help without seeing the fall. Yet stopping the process starts with enlightenment of a strict sort.

Consider these fascinating statistics:

- Some 43 percent of Americans acknowledged in a recent survey that they would fall for a guaranteed-return investment scam.
- Nearly two-thirds of online adults believe it is illegal to charge different people different prices, a practice retailers call price customization.
- Customers are often unaware of basic consumer protection laws. For example, one-third of consumers questioned after credit card reforms were recently enacted believed the laws offered two protections that they didn't. (It is a cap, for the first time, on "late fees" and a 20 percent limit on interest rates, should you care.)

Should it be this way? I can't believe you're asking me. No, the first step to knowledge is confusion and an admission that we don't know a hill of beans. In a survey I like to quote, a paltry 59 percent of Americans as a whole described themselves as highly—or very— knowledgeable when it comes to personal finance, down from 64 percent two years earlier. Maybe we could all use some help to be enlightened.

In the previous chapter, I outlined the responsibilities that you the customer must face. After all, how can you begin to be a responsible consumer if you don't even know what the rare bird looks like? Achieving enlightenment requires you to develop an unquenchable thirst for education (think Adult School for Shopping). If you want to buy right, put yourself in the business's shoes and turn the tables by adopting those strategies pursued by the smartest customers. It requires that you short-circuit your reflexes and curb your subconscious mind, both of which demand that you *buy, buy, buy!* Reflexes don't care if you're making an irrational decision. You do.

A Thirst for Knowledge

Here's a short list of sites that can lead to a better understanding of consumer issues.

Better Business Bureau: https://www.bbb.org/blog/

Consumer Reports (subscription required): www.consumerreports .org

Consumerist: www.consumerist.com

The Consumer Chronicle: http://www.theconsumerchronicle.com/

Consumer World: http://consumerworld.org/

Daily Finance: www.dailyfinance.com

The Red Tape Chronicles: http://redtape.msnbc.msn.com/

Smart Money: http://www.smartmoney.com/

That's your starting point. Follow these consumer news sources, and soon you'll be discovering your own. These media outlets are growing as primary sources for other mainstream media coverage of consumer issues, which means that if there's a scam out there you'll read about it on one of these sites first. That's a departure from the media landscape a decade ago, when you'd have to search big newspapers and often had to pay for the privilege. What a difference a couple of years makes to the savvy shopper.

When I was in college, one of my journalism professors required her students to read three newspapers and keep a log of our daily activity. "Why three?" I asked her privately one day.

"It's not the newspapers," she explained. "I want to get you into the habit of reading the *news* daily."

At the time I didn't recognize the brilliance of the exercise. A thousand years later, I get it. This practice should apply not only to newspapers but to every type of media—social networks like Google+, Facebook, Twitter, plus blogs, podcasts, newsletters, trade rags—you get the point. The more news you consume the less chance you'll be swindled. (Granted, you can't consume information uncritically, otherwise you'll fall for some of the nonsense planted by, *gasp*, unethical publicists. I assume you can spot that trend handily.)

Getting Inside the Mind of a Business

Understanding how businesses work doesn't require an MBA, and you don't even need Economics 101, though Home Economics helps. All you should know about the corporate mind is this: no matter what big corporations say or do, they are out to make money. Although this may sound obvious to the naked reader, it really isn't. Most customers expect a business and its employees to respond to situations in roughly the same way they do. And then they wake up.

He Said/She Said

Like Mars and Venus, customers and companies don't always get one another. You may be saying one thing, but like masters and dogs, someone is usually hearing something else.

What You Say	*What They Hear*
"I'd like a refund."	"Thanks for the freebie."
"When does this item go on sale?"	"I'm cheap."
"Do you have layaway?"	"I can't afford your product and besides I'm not a serious buyer."
"What's your URL?"	"I'll find the same product online for less."
"Who is your supervisor?"	"I'm going over your head to do better, you 'order taker'!"

Corporatespeak

The following is jargon that businesses use in your presence and what they *really* mean.

Bandwidth. A term for resources, specifically time. "I don't have the bandwidth for that" means they're too busy for *you*. Really, when someone mentions limited bandwidth, this has nothing to do with high-speed connectivity; they feel you're not that important. Others deserve their oh-so-valuable time. As if.

Consumercentric. Synonym for "we love our customers," and it means "we will do whatever it takes to please you." Highly unlikely. Remember what Shakespeare said, kinda. "They doth protest too much!" It's a sign to walk out or close your browser.

Outside the box. A clichéd and probably unsanctioned resolution to a problem. It usually has nothing to do with the packaging or the way it's produced. Everyone thinks they do everything uniquely, thus hardly anything is that creative.

Transparent. Another word for "open and honest." In the rare instance when a business shows you the price it's paying for the product (i.e., its cost), this is being transparent. In most cases, I find when a company boasts of transparency, it's waving, "I lie."

Sustainable. Outside the business world *sustainable* means environmentally friendly—something that can be produced into another product in a second or third life. However, within the corporate society it's the business that is being sustained. Be sure that brands explain which one they mean when referring to a product as "sustainable." And if they start talking about how green they are, remind them what Kermit said about how difficult that is to maintain.

Win-win. A common term that says you and the business benefit the most from the transaction. However, a *true* "win-win" is rare. Most are "win-lose" transactions. And guess who loses? It's not the company.

Spend any amount of time visiting corporate headquarters and speaking with executives, and it's clear that those folks see us differently from the way we see ourselves. It is all too easy to objectify people who are customers, referring to them as "sales" or "prospects." But this book isn't about making companies appreciate our perspective. They won't.

One of the most common refrains you hear when talking with a company is how they're "not a charity." Sure they're not. But there are plenty of orgs, including nonprofits, philanthropic groups, and political entities that also want to raise money—and they *are* charities. So essentially some company reminding us how charity doesn't begin with them sharpens the focus in one heck of a way. That means all pretenses of niceness—indeed, of conscience—are gone. That corporate employee who mutters "Well, we're not . . . " is now admitting that the business for which she works is a money-making machine with an overtly singular purpose of creating wealth for its bosses, owners, and shareholders. Customers are a necessary, if not entirely evil, means to an end. As you've heard me lecture, that's how a free market economy works. That's capitalism. It is the consumer's duty to remember and work around the fog that tries to cloud these truths.

Customers Behaving Badly

I've had a front-row seat to bold-faced unenlightened consumer behavior, and it's not pretty. Consumers often forget the basic stuff like read the contract, count the change, and do a little research. Yes, I know I've said that. I'm reminding you because now you get to see some that are shockers.

- *Open the box, please.* Be sure you actually open the product. One U.K. supermarket customer didn't and dialed its customer service number in an angry huff: "It's just bread, no toppings," he said, demanding that the company send him a takeout pizza to replace the one he'd purchased. During the call, he flipped the frozen pizza over to reveal that everything was where it should be; he just opened it the wrong way around. The call was recorded and leaked onto YouTube for posterity.
- *Go postal on them.* Melodi Dushane got some bad news when she arrived at a McDonald's drive-through in Toledo, Ohio: chicken nuggets aren't served for breakfast. Wrong answer! Dushane jumped out of the car, slugged the worker, and then smashed a window. She was sentenced to 60 days behind bars. Maybe she should have ordered the Happy Meal.
- *Have a tantrum (my favorite—like being a kid).* When a passenger on a Cathay Pacific flight missed her plane, she went ultra-ballistic. The 50ish woman charged a security guard at the departure gate, screaming at the top of her lungs in a rant that lasted, oh, about three minutes. The video went "viral" online. Curiously, she was allowed to board the next flight. She should be glad *I* wasn't in charge.

Expecting an employee to bend a rule for you out of the goodness of his heart is like asking for better weather. So what if you want it? After all, employees are not trained to help you save money; they're trained to make sales—no sales and no job—and to fulfill the mission of every entity that puts its hands out: *to make money.*

One of my blog participants, Claudia Krich, recently contacted me about a purchase of a Nikon camera. Over the years, her family has owned numerous cameras and other gadgets from Nikon, and they were always pleased—that is, until now.

Krich bought an inexpensive Nikon Coolpix L22 camera. "My husband had been using it for about a week there when, as he was about to take a picture, he noticed the screen went half-white," she said. "It was the strangest thing because it just spontaneously happened."

The Kriches—who had paid about $100 for the digital camera—insisted that they had done nothing to harm it. "It had not been dropped, smashed, kicked, or hit," she told me.

Initially, Nikon offered to fix it for half the price of repair—about $50, not including shipping. Krich declined. "They said it wasn't covered by the warranty, because we had caused it to happen. But the fact is, we didn't," she told me.

It's unclear what caused Krich's camera to display the half white. What *is* evident is that these long-time customers were unhappy with the camera and were just a click away from defecting to Canon.

I contacted Nikon on Claudia Krich's behalf, thinking this was all a misunderstanding. After all, the Kriches hadn't done anything to the camera. I was surprised when the company rejected me outright. "The LCD on the camera screen is cracked," a company spokesman told me. "This [occurs] due to an impact and is not something that just happens . . . as it requires a good amount of force or impact for this to [take place]. Whether or not the Kriches are aware of what happened, this type of damage is not covered under our warranty."

Gee. Replacing a camera would be a simple way to make a long-time customer happy. But it appeared the customer service person was trained to maximize shareholder value no matter what, so "no" was the default response. Kind of like a five-year-old!

The lesson from the broken Nikon isn't just a shortsighted manufacturer with too-stringent rules in a world gone flexible. My point is, just saying "no way" to anything is not going to make the shareholders more money in the long run. This is what the customer learns on the way to enlightenment.

Getting Inside Your Head

We know the various ways money-oriented companies target your unconscious mind with sales pitches. Even as I write this, smart businesses are developing new tactics to persuade you to buy—by using sharpened methods like subliminal messaging, aural fixes, or specialized lighting, or store design that makes you feel you *should* make a purchase you probably don't need or even want.

The best way to fight off such techniques is to learn as much as you can. Assume that no matter how friendly or cool the site you're on is, someone is selling to you (even on *Consumer Reports,* which does a hard sell for its sister publication, the not inexpensive *Shop Smart* magazine, on nearly every page). You're being marketed to *everywhere.* Someone hands you something at the mall, you "find" a card inside a copy shop. Assume it's all meant to sell. What's that line about never getting a free lunch? It's never been more true than here, in this world of schemes, swindles, and shady deals. And you may be the savviest shopper and hold your wallet on a tight leash, but you can bet your subconscious is making a decision with or without the *conscious* you consenting.

Not falling prey to these sophisticated marketing techniques means avoiding picking from the best vantage point on a sales floor (the most expensive are on the aisle or, in the grocery store, at face view) as well as making yourself aware of the behind-the-scenes activity. You want to make buying decisions in a neutral place that you control. For example, if you think you might be in the market for a car, it's better to steer yourself away from the showroom floor where the dealers are waiting for a mark, floodlights trained on the cars they need to get rid of. Ah, the dealership, where a barrage of time-tested stimuli is intended to get you to drive out of there today. I say, think about it at home. Do research, make a decision, force your way in—and demand satisfaction.

How Successful Customers Think

I spend my day talking to consumers who have had both successful and unsuccessful experiences. My conversations with them have helped me compile the following list of how the best shoppers think.

- *They're curious in every color.* Good customers are always asking, "Why?" They're kicking tires and inquiring about the specs, the contract, the warranty (not extended, but expected). They know that the more questions they ask, the better buying decision they make.
- *They compare.* Savvy buyers compare products instinctively. They judge one brand or one product against another almost incessantly, both before and during their purchasing process. Ask a 10-year-old, who spends most of his time on the Web, whether he'd buy *anything* without first knowing about what else is available. Go ahead, I'll wait.
- *They can't get enough of that ol' information.* Consumers in the know devour words and video from mainstream and social media. I've found they get involved by leaving comments with their own buying experiences; that's just karma. And, for what it's worth, they also hold bloggers like me accountable when we get it wrong. Which we do.
- *They pay attention to detail.* Everything in life comes to those who look closely and inspect before nodding yes. They pay attention to price, read the microprint on the end-user agreements, file away every single receipt, and remember the name of the salesperson they dealt with—especially on the phone or online. (This is a good reason to archive e-mails instead of deleting.)
- *They remember everything.* If you work in a store and sell one of these smarties a dud, they will hold that memory for years to come. These people are known as happy bigmouths. They spend every waking moment telling anyone who will listen

(continued)

(*continued*)

about the bad service they received. On the positive side, if they buy a product they like or love, they will shout to the rooftops about how wonderful the experience was.

■ *They cannot live by price alone.* Yes, some super successful consumers are professional coupon clippers, but they know when to use one and when one is not worth even a penny. A low price (even one that's subsidized, or whose cost is lower because the company expects to make up the loss by selling something else) can't be the primary purpose for a purchase. Good customers look for quality, service, and price—a triple threat!

What Smart Shoppers *Don't* Do

A recent survey by MasterCard was purported to reveal what these smart shoppers do. It's interesting to compare what customers believe makes them clever to what enlightened consumers *actually* do.

■ *Purchase gift certificates or gift cards for holiday gifts (53 percent).* Since many gift certificates either expire or depreciate in value, they are almost *always* a bad deal. Think of it as someone putting a time limit on your own money. When the time's up, the business gets to keep your dollars, whether or not you've gotten anything from them in return.

■ *Shopping online (34 percent).* True, you can sometimes find lower prices online; but with no store, you're also missing important services like having a person to talk to when you have a question or a place to take the product back.

■ *Shopping in store for early bird specials (30 percent).* You mean, jump at an offer before you've had a chance to read the reviews and talk with other customers about what they think of the product? Oh, *that* sounds smart! (On the other hand, if you've done your homework and know what you want, it could be a reasonably good deal.)

■ *Waiting for last-minute deals (28 percent)*. This one is a favorite of the travel industry, where products like rooms and airline seats are considered a perishable commodity. If a plane flies with an empty seat, an airline gets nothing for it. But waiting until the eleventh hour can be a dangerous game if you absolutely need this thing.

Being a victim is not inevitable, and neither is being ignorant. With a little information—and by taking time to see how a business feels about you—you become savvier. You can also understand why businesses try to disrupt your common sense with efforts to get inside your purse or wallet. It's a trait within the corporate beast.

But true enlightenment is hard. The path is littered with bona fide scams that cannot be seen until, unfortunately, they've hit you square in the bank account. Here's what to look for next.

12

It's Dangerous Out There

The first and worst of all frauds is to cheat oneself.

—Philip James Bailey

WHEN YOU'VE BEEN scammed, you'll encounter a predictable series of emotions, including denial, guilt, and resignation. Mostly you'll be ticked-off. Even today, years after I've forgotten most of the details of the pyramid scheme I fell for years ago, I'm still filled with rage when I think about it—mostly at myself for being taken.

In 1989, I was invited to attend an "investment seminar" by an elderly affluent couple, family friends for years. The pitch that evening was unlike anything I'd ever witnessed. The auditorium near the office park was packed with well-dressed, successful-seeming types. Onstage, men in designer suits made polished presentations in which they guaranteed us "automatic" six-figure incomes within weeks of signing. The audience cheered loudly. Looking back I realize that most of them—including the people who dragged, uh, took me there—were likely the early investors looking to make money by signing up newbies. The fact that I could escape $3,000 lighter (that's $5,400 in today's money) was a miracle. This, friends, was a cult of people pulling money from others. I consider myself unscathed by this shady "investment." My sister, who against my sage advice became even more deeply immersed in a similar pyramid some time later, was just one "level" away from those who went to prison, which is the line that separates the scammers from the scammed.

The scheme I'd fallen for collapsed within a few months, as all do, and my fellow suckers lost their investments, too, often tens or hundreds of thousands of pre-Madoff dollars. But I consider this three grand tuition for learning one of life's most crucial lessons. After that event, even the pyramid on a dollar bill looked suspicious.

Some thieves are obvious; you experience that painful moment when you know you've been taken, and the lingering anger is a powerful reminder that prevents it from happening to you again, as with my minor stupidity. However, the best scams are much more cleverly structured, siphoning from you slowly and in small sums, so discreetly that they fail to arouse your suspicions.

In our nation, businesses don't want you to think anything is a scam. They'd prefer you consider the money you spend as simple consumer "choices."

Everywhere a Scam

It's difficult to determine the exact number of victims to indecent strategies because there's no agreement on the definition of the word *scam*. The government institution that should know, namely the Federal Trade Commission (FTC), conducted a statistical survey of fraud in the United States in 2007 that suggested 30.2 million Americans (or 13.5 percent of the adult population) were victims of fraud during the previous year.

The Most Common Scams

- Fraudulent Weight-Loss Products (4.8 million victims)
- Foreign Lottery Scams (3.2 million victims)
- Unauthorized Billing—Buyers Clubs (3.2 million victims)
- Prize Promotions (2.7 million victims)
- Work-at-Home Programs (2.4 million victims)
- Credit Card Insurance (2.1 million victims)

- Unauthorized Billing—Internet Services (1.8 million victims)
- Advance-Fee Loans (1.7 million victims)
- Credit Repair Scams (1.2 million victims)
- Business Opportunities (.8 million victims)

But these are what I would call lowercase scams—the ones that are easily identified and stopped. The uppercase scams are simply tough to ascertain and even harder to end, and the ones I've outlined in the earlier sections are even more difficult to quantify.

How to Spot a Lowercase Scam

In order to understand how to deal with uppercase scams, we first have to spend a little time on the lowercase scams, because the two are closely related.

Lyn Cacella found an unbelievably good deal on a Royal Caribbean cruise to Bermuda through a site she'd never heard of (and wishes that remained so) named GlobalCruisesOnSale.com. The catch? She had to wire $1,359 to the business for her fare.

Yes, her tickets did not arrive so she, trusting soul, phoned the cruise line, which had no record of her reservation. When she e-mailed the folks at GlobalCruisesOnSale about the preponderance of bad reviews it had gotten, she was referred to another site, this time BuySecureOnline.org, which "certified" the business as legitimate.

"I think it's a hoax," she said.

Cacella's cruise to nowhere was in fact a textbook scam and she never got her money back. Here are a few telltale signs something is amiss:

- *You've never heard of the company business, or it has a ridiculous-sounding name.* If you don't know the company, it could be a scam. If no one you know has heard of it either, there's an even better chance that this is the case. And if you can't find any information about it online—good, bad, or otherwise—just run away. I receive e-mails every week asking me if I've heard of a particular company offering a sweet deal. Good businesses leave a trail of happy customers; bad businesses simply cover tracks. A fraudulent enterprise makes it difficult to impossible to contact them; a site without a phone number to call is probably being run in someone's smelly cellar.

- *Speaking of which, the business doesn't pass the sniff test.* Most scams look too good to be true. That's because they *are* too good to be true. Trust your instincts. They are usually right.

- *The firm wants you to pay by cash, money order, or—worse—certified check.* Everyone with an iPad can accept a credit card now. (Some exceptions apply. Except in Beverly Hills, hot dog vending may be a cash-only business, but where would we be without the franks?) Beware of a company that sells big-ticket items like TVs, cruises, or cars but that somehow doesn't take plastic. And if they want you to wire, tell them to take a hike. You can't dispute such a transaction if something goes wrong. Once an unscrupulous business has your money, it's over. (Also, check that your credit card company will allow you to dispute charges; if it does not, get rid of it.)

- *Someone insistently asks for personal information like a credit card number or your mother's maiden name via e-mail.* No legitimate business demands anything this way. If it isn't a real form that you are filling out, with a TRUST-E verification on the cart page, this is definitely a scam. Don't share personal data via e-mail.

- *They're asking you to buy right now.* Shady sales ventures apply high-pressure tactics, claiming they're offering you the last available unit in a timeshare or that, gee, there's only one more car model on the lot. (It's like QVC saying "We have four left! Only four!" This is never factual, and it's more like 400.) Such tactics are questionable, and usually mean there's a problem, Houston. They may also worry that you'll start to compare their products to a competitor's. Take your time; don't hurry. Remember what your momma told you about shopping around.

- *They're offering something for "free." Free* is a misnomer in almost all cases. If a business says something is free, you shouldn't have to shell out anything for it. Most of the scams I deal with start with a free offer and then make you buy something—or worse, give tons of personal information that is really worth a lot. This is an ages-old bait-and-switch game that signals a problem—the product or service is likely a lot less than you are expecting.

■ *They condescendingly tell you not to worry your pretty little head about the contract.* The most accomplished scam artists assure you the contract is simply a formality or send you the *Reader's Digest* version, or a one-size-fits-all boilerplate that everyone signs. Yeah, right. If you can't use it in court, it's not worth the thin paper you use to print.

How many of these signs applied to Cacella's cruise? More than you'd think. I contacted Royal Caribbean to find out what, if anything, they knew about GlobalCruisesOnSale.Com. The answer? Nothing. Royal Caribbean referred the matter to its legal department, which sent GlobalCruisesOnSale.com a Cease & Desist letter. Before I could redial anyone, both the offending site and its sister thief, BuySecureOnline.org, went dark. Which you saw coming.

Scammy Businesses?

Industries with the Lowest Service Scores as of 2011

Rank	Industry	Score/Grade
1.	Airlines	65/D
2.	Newspapers	65/D (tie)
3.	Subscription television service	66/D
4.	Wireless telephone service	71/D
5.	Motion pictures	73/D
6.	Fixed-line phone service	73/D
7.	Cellular telephones	75/C
8.	Hospitals	77/C
9.	Network cable TV news	77/C
10.	Computer software	78/C
11.	Limited service restaurants	79/C

Source: The American Customer Satisfaction Index.
Note: Scores are on a scale of 1–100. I added a letter grade.

Does bad service mean you're getting scammed? Maybe. Usually it's a serious indicator light revealing that a business has little or no respect for customers and would pull a fast one if it could get away with it. Airlines and, ahem, newspapers are just one minus from a failing grade, and a lot of people who fall under those categories are serious offenders. Sadly, these are two fields with distinguished track records of taking their customers for granted. I take no pleasure in disclosing this because I'm a former newspaper guy and someone who has covered aviation.

Airlines are de facto monopolies with über-powerful lobbies that include the Federal Aviation Administration. These constantly merging entities have not been incentivized to provide decent service since deregulation in the 1970s. The newspaper industry has been slower than a scared turtle to innovate; people who read the biggies get the feeling the news conglomerate is doing them a huge favor. With that disregard, other, more caring news sites have claimed once-loyal readers. (For example, if you e-mail a columnist at the *New York Times*, you land on a form that says these "letters" will be shared at a certain time each morning. In what century?)

The next-worst category is entertainment, namely pay TV, cinema and DVD, and wireless phone companies. I include wireless in the group because a lot of smartphones are more about entertainment than communicating these days.

There is no need for me to go on a rant about the quality of movies and TV. I can be as critical as the next guy. Ah, and how about cable companies, another form of walled garden that limits choice, keeps prices high, and has the audacity to show you an ad before a movie that you've already paid for? Pathetic.

Communication services—now here's another business with high fees and unbearably bad service. I mean, can you remember the last time your wireless call was dropped? Or when you saw a suspicious charge on your bill? Maybe your carrier "crammed" that surcharge onto your bill, a practice that became so widespread in the industry that the feds had to intervene in 2011 by imposing tough new rules on an industry that's unaccustomed to the heavy hand of government regulation. Telecoms have some of the biggest lobbyists working to ensure they can have their way with the customer. As for the AT&T and T-Mobile merger, in a normal world that would not be allowed. Welcome to Fantasyland.

As a consumer advocate I say take a stance like Howard Beale in the classic *Network* and say you've had enough. Put your foot down. A little bit of fight goes a long way.

How to Spot an Uppercase Scam

The big scams that smartypants corporations perpetrate are frequently too sophisticated to detect without a microscope.

In order to understand the designs of these masters of deception, first study the clumsy tactics of the amateurs that are trying to emulate them. We've already seen how big companies can manipulate customers with clever search-engine wizardry, corporate spin, and unorthodox promotions. It would be nearly impossible to calculate how much "bank" these corporations have amassed using these underhanded stratagems, but out-of-the-ballpark estimates by those who've studied the trend say it ranges well into tens of billions and maybe more. We see how they do it. But how do we catch them before it costs us?

Throughout this book, I've talked about the times I was scammed. I always figured it out—they were obvious instances. But the perfect crime is, ask Miss Marple, the one they get away with. What if a vast populace of victims had no clue they were being swindled and just kept on acting as if the sun was shining on their purchases? What if we consumers were actually helping companies perpetuate these uppercase scams by our complicity as we wallow in the complacency of those prisoned gardens, unknowingly making others richer by own inertia and neglect? Yes, what if?

Here's how uppercase scams at face value differ from their lowercase brothers.

You know who's taking advantage of you. Bigger scams are committed by major brands with established reputations. These mammoths commit these acts in plain sight because—thanks to lobbyists and high-power politician friends—these immoral activities are totally within the law. The one tipoff that something is wrong in Corporateville is the record profits being recorded by the public companies that occur year after year. And in a recession, no less.

- *Something smells . . . good.* Uppercase scams have learned to cover the bad smell by distracting you. These are done with subliminal, hardly noticeable marketing to override your sense that something is going awry.
- *Credit card? PayPal? IOU? No problem!* Because uppercase scams are long-term and perpetrated by "legitimate" businesses, they offer all payment options. Why? Because they know the credit card companies, who won't fight something that makes *them* wealthier, will support an uppercase scam until someone actually points it out.
- *They run by the book.* During a scam by a real operator, everything appears *to be perfectly legit.* They'll never ask you to reveal personal information in a way that compromises your privacy. But a scam is a scam is a scam. Apologies to Gertrude Stein.
- *No pressure.* Because high-pressure sales tactics are dead giveaways of a con to everyone who isn't simply naïve, uppercase scammers work with their employees to practice the art of the soft sell. They help you find "solutions" to your "challenges" with their products. Remember the Elliott motto that businesses are there to *help you* by *helping themselves* to your money.
- *"You get what you pay for."* Uppercase scam-companies will generally shy away from offering anything gimmicky—nothing free here. They prefer to talk about "quality" and how you're getting what you expect from your final payment. Rhetoric like that can be evidence of mischief of a high order.
- *Go on, read the contract.* Businesses that have perfected the scam have ironclad, suspiciously complicated contracts written by in-house lawyers who aren't paid by the hour. They welcome your amateur attempts to make sense of the legalese; even some lawyers can't. Besides, it isn't how you interpret it that matters; as always it's how a court rules. And these companies usually have quite an outrageous record when it comes to winning.

Even when you're dealing with pros who have run uppercase scams their entire career, there are warning signs that can stop these from reaching you. One of the catalysts of the 2008 financial crisis was an unsustainable real estate bubble. History proved that home prices were rising faster than anyone could afford. Any intelligent consumer who thought about it without wincing and could project the growth rate of his own home a few years in advance could see that no way could this go on indefinitely.

What's the actual difference between an uppercase scam like the frothy real estate market and a lowercase scam like the pyramid scheme that ensnared me? It's in the marketing sleight of hand. The real estate bubble had cheerleaders with PhDs and Pulitzers—with a lot to gain from it. The lowly pyramid scheme I fell for merely had some suits who'd majored in Lying.

And while it took months for reality to catch up with the Southern California scammers who snookered me, years went by before the real estate bubble popped and Americans woke to the foggy morning of our collective greed. Ironically, the same people who enriched themselves at our expense in the 2000s are still fabulously wealthy and planning their next move. That's nothing to shrug off.

How to Save Money

I've read a lot of great books that offer very specific advice about how to spot and avoid a scam. While most of them deal with lowercase scams in the guise of a bad mortgage, automobile purchase, or investment, they all have something in common: the voice in a customer's head usually saying, "Something's not quite right." You will hear that voice if you slow down before pulling the proverbial trigger.

How to Deflect a Clever Sales Pitch

Whether it's an established place selling you a questionable product or some dude on a street corner hawking a faux TV, it all begins with the offer to you. So how do you say no to the effective pitch?

Let's look at the most aggressive, shameless salespeople in the world: off-property consultants (OPCs), who sell timeshares via slick presentations. When I wanted to figure out how to short-circuit the sales process, I knew the person to go to was Lisa Ann Schreier, a timeshare industry insider and author of *Timeshare Vacations for Dummies*.

"OPCs can be very forward," she told me. For example, they're known to approach you on the street or the beach, in restaurants and near your home, and offer you anything from theme park tickets to free helicopter rides—but always something in a great location—in exchange for attending a "90-minute presentation." But the benefits rarely materialize and if they do, it's after you've spent at least two hours being lulled by sales pushes and hype. That in *itself* is a scam.

What's more, OPCs don't give a hoot if you're happy with your purchase. They collect anywhere from $10 to more than $100 per head as referral fees, and since you're away from your day-to-day, these people know how to play on your vacation sensibilities. Plus, they'll never see you again.

How do you survive this sales encounter? Don't do it! Timeshare OPCs target tourists like those on International Drive in Orlando and along the beaches of Cancun. If you want to avoid being pitched, stay away from these locales—or be prepared for a possible confrontation. And if you are confronted, have a really great answer at the ready.

- "I'm leaving tomorrow."
- "I've already been to a timeshare presentation."
- "We're trying to sell our timeshare."
- And failing everything, "Get out of my face!"

Whatever it is—and threatening to find a policeman is usually best—have your response prepared if you're late for an important date. You can actually apply this advice to any sales situation, whatever the product. A quick riposte that catches the predator off guard is as close to a firewall against this swindle as you can get. (I usually say "Must go home; my bathroom's on fire," and no one can retort.) Here are two simple responses:

1. *Slow down.* Effective sales pitches rely on momentum; make a decision now, and if you don't, *oops* the offer's off the table. Therefore, "Don't make a decision in haste," explained Lisa Ann Schreier. When you react fast, momentum favors the salesperson. It's often funny how quickly the scammer will wave goodbye if you insist on reading the fine print or say you want to think about the offer overnight—the worst for them is "I need to discuss it

with my spouse"—because no decent scam can withstand scrutiny or a good night's sleep. They are fast-talkers and will do whatever it takes to get you to act now. Remember, these people have a quota. Don't become a stat. Simply put, don't do it.

2. *Just say no.* See, Nancy Reagan was right. Saying no can be a lot more difficult than it sounds because most of us were brought up to have manners, and it's rude to not let someone finish. Salespeople, especially those hawking timeshares, are trained to exploit our good selves. (By the way, since we're talking timeshares, I'd exercise extreme caution when considering one. They can come with hidden fees, unreasonable rules, and depreciate over time. They're almost always a bad investment, in my view.) Those who say yes are usually in for a world of hurt. I have counseled many a heartbroken vacationer who was slurping margaritas on the beach one minute and writing a check for $25,000 to an aggressor the next. The negative answer would have spared them their grief— and they could have finished that drink.

And what if you answer yes? Well, that's what every business-person wants, and it's true if we just stopped buying, the economy would implode. No one is advocating that we stop making all purchases—only the fraudulent ones. As Schreier advocated, "Make sure you understand what you're buying."

Surviving a Scam

Scams are all around us, and we can't turn down every pitch. But unlike the lowercase scams that offer scant choices for retribution— meaning you contact the law or file a suit—there are a wider range of options available to combat uppercase scams. In order to do that, you'll have to work with what's euphemistically called customer service. Most customer service departments are neither about the customer or its service; they're there to make you go away and keep the business going for as long as possible. Let's end the cycle now.

13

The I-Can't-Help-Desk

However impenetrable it seems, if you don't try it, then you can never do it.

—Andrew Wiles

I'M AT THE end of my rope. I'm trying to download a few transactions from my bank to my computer early on a Saturday morning, but I've been placed on hold for 15 and 20 minutes at a time, and I've spoken with several so-called customer service representatives who don't seem to understand a word I'm saying. It's like English as a Second Language—with the students running the class. (Rep: "Please to click on Start, All Programs." Me: "I'm on a Mac. There's no Start button." Rep: "Yes, Start. Please *click* Start.") This is two hours of my life, and I'm no closer to a fix. My Saturday morning is shot.

I'm in help desk hell. (Cue *Outer Limits* music.)

You've been there and are nodding your head. What you might not realize is that the 800 number you dial, which is often referred to as the help desk or the customer-service number—is there primarily to persuade you to go away and accept the product about which you're calling to complain. Customer relief is the fake part of an impressive

On Hold Forever

By the Numbers

55 seconds: The average hold time for a business with more than two phone lines

60 percent: Callers who are placed on hold who then hang up

30 percent: Callers who hang up who never call back

machine that includes the company site, offshore call center, service agents, and a social-media team that is tasked with helping a company keep its often ill-gotten profits.

I have a lifetime of experience being on hold with companies, as do the people I try to assist. We are all outraged by the long wait times, and we universally believe that companies intentionally force us into the waiting game to get rid of us. And we are right.

The first thing to understand is that companies usually *want* you to use the phone when you have a question or complaint about a product. The phone remains the number-one way customers contact a company, and it's true that phones are more convenient, even in the age of e-mail, texting, and the all-powerful blog, tweet, and status update. However, there's another reason: There's no tangible record of a phone call, at least on the customer's side. I know what you're thinking: "Wait a sec. 'This call *is* being recorded for quality assurance', right, Chris?" My answer: "Prove it."

Consider Dawn Lyon's problem with notable customer service failure, Sprint. She flew to Vancouver for a business meeting, but before leaving called the wireless carrier to find out the most efficient way to connect in a foreign land, which at this writing Canada remains. That's always good practice.

"The agent noted I already had an international plan and that would make me eligible for reduced priced calls," she says.

Lyon specifically asked about the recently purchased MiFi, a wireless hotspot connected to several devices. "He said I didn't need to worry about the MiFi," Lyon remembers. "He said, 'It's just like in the U.S.'"

Au contraire.

"When I returned to the U.S., I was advised both my phone—and most notably, my MiFi—had nearly $800 in data roaming charges for a weekend," she exclaimed.

So began her adventure of trying to reduce that huge bill. After several hours of phone nonsense with Sprint, a representative agreed to trim her bill by 15 percent. Not enough. After more haggling, a supervisor cut it to 50 percent.

Couldn't Sprint pull up a recording of the call she had with the rep back when? Not possible, she was told.

As I reviewed her correspondence with Sprint, it seemed the company actually *wanted* her to use the phone rather than put anything in writing. A cynic might conclude it wanted to ensure there was no record of the correspondence—so there would be no legal standing to speak of (pun intended). Sprint should have continued the conversation via e-mail, which would have established a paper trail of her grievance, but I live to imagine such things.

I reviewed her correspondence and thought Sprint only had a few options: Either it promised her that MiFi wouldn't incur any roaming charges and shouldn't have charged her $800, or Lyon had baked up the conversation and ought to pay up. There's no third way—no splitting the difference—on this one. Either Sprint is right, or it's not.

I contacted Sprint, and it investigated Lyon's grievance. It eventually apologized to her for any information that may have been relayed inaccurately and adjusted the bill to her satisfaction. "We are also working to fully educate the customer service agent about roaming charges in the future," a company spokeswoman told me.

They did right, but talk is cheap. If you don't have written proof of an offer, the company is off the hook. Which is clever. When it comes to cell mobile phone company profits, all roads lead to "roam."

How to Escape from Call Center Hell

Once you've dialed—and yes, even pushing buttons is considered "dialing"—you're almost certain to end up in some variation of

Longest Hold Times

The following is a list of online companies with the longest hold times:

Rank	Company	"Hold" Time
1.	BN.com	8 minutes, 3 seconds
2.	CSNStores.com	7 minutes, 20 seconds
3.	Macys.com	7 minutes, 12 seconds
4.	Zones.com	6 minutes, 56 seconds
5.	GreenMountainCoffee.com	4 minutes, 50 seconds
6.	Buy.com	4 minutes, 30 seconds
7.	Costco.com	4 minutes, 21 seconds
8.	CrateandBarrel.com	4 minutes, 10 seconds
9.	HPShopping.com	4 minutes, 6 seconds
10.	Avon.com	3 minutes, 49 seconds

And here are the brick-and-mortar companies with the longest "hold" times:

Rank	Company	"Hold" Time
1.	Continental Airlines (now United Airlines)	13 minutes
2.	Air Canada	10 minutes
3.	IRS (Personal)	9 minutes
4.	Amtrak	9 minutes
5.	AT&T Customer Service (General)	8 minutes
6.	Delta Air Lines	7 minutes
7.	Southwest Airlines	7 minutes
8.	JetBlue Airways	6 minutes
9.	ACE Hardware	6 minutes
10.	AARP Healthcare	5 minutes

Help Desk Hell. A truly infernal example of how long you could be put on hold—though you will probably never get such a test—is that of Tonya Davis of Rainham, England, who was just trying to unfreeze her Internet connection when she phoned Virgin Media at 11 P.M. one evening. She went to bed listening to hold music. When she woke up after a decent night's sleep, she was still on hold, same droning music. According to Davis, Virgin answered the phone at 11 A.M.

When she told a supervisor about her lengthy hold time, he said, shocked: "Oh my God, seriously?"

Here are some of the places you might end up—and how to escape from them.

- *Phone tree purgatory.* "Please listen to the entire message as our menu options have changed." That's always how it starts. It ends with you angrily stabbing the "0" button until your finger turns blue, then finally disconnecting the call. "Whew," says the company. Phone trees serve a legitimate purpose: to sort calls by subject. Unfortunately, they also deflect through automation millions of legitimate complaints a year. Most customers simply give up and hang up.
- *Spending an eternity on hold.* During peak call times—like lunch or after work—you can expect to spend an hour or more in a hold queue. Punching "zero" won't help, and in fact often sets you back to the beginning of the phone tree where you hear, "I'm sorry, I did not understand your request." But there is a little-known shortcut which a call center trainer (who requested anonymity) recently shared with me. Most large companies offer a Spanish option—"Para Espanol, marque dos." "Go ahead and press two," says the insider. "At this point, you'll be transferred into Spanish-speaking queues for all departments within the organization you are calling. Just hit '0' a few times and you will get a representative. They will answer in Spanish, so just go ahead and start speaking in English with your problem." Don't tell the rep that you intentionally hit the Spanish option. The call center workers are all bilingual, and the wait times are almost always shorter for Spanish-speaking customers.

A second helpful, crafty hint is to push the button for new customers, people that haven't been indoctrinated into the horror of its service. They will answer quickly and cheerily and you will begin talking through your problem; do not let them transfer you. Everybody can help.

■ *Script-reading inferno.* Scripts are a necessary part of call centers, because they guide representatives on how to deal with a problem. When operators face an issue they've never handled, they can turn to the PC and get step-by-step instructions. But overreliance on scripts can turn the call center worker into a reading robot—which can quickly drive you crazy. If an operator is repeating your questions, giving you answers that sound like questions, pausing between answers, or if it sounds as if you're being read to, odds are you're in script-reading inferno. Getting out is easy: Ask for that person's supervisor. Not just *a* supervisor but *that* person's supervisor. Chances are you'll be transferred to someone whose job is to speak in their own words.

■ *The rejection.* The final insult, of course, is being turned down. Call center workers have a hundred ways to reject you, but their favorite is to say no without actually *saying* it. Promising to get back to you on an issue is a favorite tactic. At a larger company, this deceptive maneuver is easy to pull off. After all, you'll never find that particular operator again (reps usually offer only their first names or a fake one and an extension, and only do so when asked). Hint: jot down as much as they're willing to part with. Establish a personal relationship—start by saying "How are you today?" Ask them about their kids. They aren't the corporation. They just work there. You have no idea how many people launch right into it without saying hello. Think about other people for a second—they may be in worse economic circumstances. A real person who thinks you are one, too, will be more sympathetic if you are kind. Together you can stick it to the bad guys.

Call center hell is just the first line of defense against your efforts to get a fair resolution to a problem, or just a simple answer to a question. Even if you make it past the phone tree, the lengthy hold time and an operator who reads from a script, you still may be turned down—or worse, given an uncertain answer or a vague promise of something that's not very likely to pan out.

Companies hope your efforts will end there, but a determined customer will see this as the beginning of the fight. The corporate society is hoping you'll take your product and leave them alone; whatever you do, they think, don't start an e-mail chain.

But that's *exactly* what you have to do.

Should You Chat?

A written grievance (or writing in general) is so much more difficult to execute than rattling off demands on the phone, even if you like to type or write. But you have to be prepared for battle and use all the tools at your disposal. Before committing to a letter, you may want to try an intermediate step that offers the benefits of the written word along with the immediacy of the spoken word: the chat. Many companies, both large and small, have a dedicated chat feature that could offer a quick resolution to a problem.

The good aspect of chat is that there is a record. There are words being typed by two people—you and them—and you can cut and paste that transcript for later use or a memento. But don't assume you will have more luck now. Sometimes you get into more misery with chat.

Consider what happened to one customer who tried to retrieve her password over chat. The experience, recalled by Forrester Research analyst Kerry Bodine, is a customer-service nightmare. Instead of concisely answering the questions, the chat employee pasted in several prewritten and poorly written answers that distracted from an easy resolution.

For example:

Remaining committed and focused on my goal which is to provide quality customer service at my fullest effort will always be at the pinnacle. It is with utmost sincerity that I want to extend apologies for any trouble, inconvenience and frustration the log in issue has brought along your way. I simply hope you are doing fine.

Then, instead of helping, this chatter tried the upsell:

Get 2 GB of space, a personalized portal, and the ability to share files. . . . Plus, you can definitely take advantage of this feature if you have Norton installed in your computer since it automatically backs up files when your PC is idle, so backups won't slow you down or get in your way. Norton Backup will back up files to the local computer.

You get the idea. Drones who just use a script can be even worse when you chat; when you need a straight answer or one that's been more carefully considered, you might want to use e-mail or even a conventional letter.

Do companies read letters in the mail? Don't you? Someone who took the time to find a stamp and an envelope often receives more attention—and higher priority—than others. But a letter via first-class Postal Service mail to the "customer service department" will *not get* as much attention as one sent "return receipt requested" right to the firm's CEO. (I'll show you how to find the name and address of a CEO in the Appendix.)

The Phone Is Dead

Is the traditional call center, with rows upon rows of cubicles filled with customer service agents, about to become a thing of the past? Maybe. A 2011 study by telecommunications firm **Avaya** suggests customers are slowly shifting their inquiries away from the phone and toward new media.

The telephone has fallen out of favor with 40 percent of international consumers, according to its survey. Most of them prefer to use other methods to interact with customer service centers such as e-mail (55 percent) and web self-serve (38 percent).

The United States is strangely behind the curve, with less than a third (32 percent) preferring the phone over these alternatives. But not for long. A majority of U.S. consumers—

56 percent—expect e-mail, text, or chat to become their regular means of contact in the next two years, and half of them say they are likely to use an automated voice response system when offered.

What does this mean? You might get better service, at least for now, staying off the phone. Companies will likely shift customer service ops to e-mail and social media methods. In a lot of cases nowadays, you do get a faster response tweeting publicly about your problem with a particular company. It's the modern-day equivalent of a display ad.

The Art of the Written Complaint

One method of communicating with a company after your purchase stands above all others: the letter, and more recently, the e-mail. And with good reason:

- *An e-mail creates a paper trail.* The company's words are documented, so there's never any question about what you were told.
- *There are auto-responders.* Companies quickly acknowledge e-mails and assign a tracking number to them—something that doesn't happen with a phone call or an in-person visit.
- *There is ease of appeal.* By clicking Forward and sending your correspondence to a manager—or a consumer advocate—you can often elicit a speedy resolution.

So how do you write the perfect letter? You start by keeping meticulous records. Retain all receipts, signed contracts, ticket stubs, and any other evidence of your purchase. For example, if your brand-new washing machine exploded in your house, don't clean up until you've taken a few digital snapshots. If you see a price that seems too good to be true online, take a screenshot. You can, and should, attach these to your initial e-mail when you're making your case or asking your question, as they're irrefutable evidence of a purchase or product defect.

These Letters Go Straight to the Trash

Some e-mails are discarded without being read. Though it varies from company to company, some rules apply.

- Letters that *contain any kind of profanity* or just come across as insane are ignored, and if you threaten someone you might get a visit from the police or the Feds. (Don't use curse words; it's f***ing unnecessary. We all get upset—be measured.)
- *USING ALL UPPERCASE in your letters* sometimes will not make it through e-mail spam filters—and the same goes for profanity-laced missives. So you're WASTING your time.
- Letters with *gratuitous file attachments* are kicked back by mail servers. Attachments contain viruses, or are suspect.
- *Asking for something so outrageous* that it doesn't merit a response is another no-no. ("My six-year-old sofa has a stain that won't come out. I want you to replace it. Now. Free.")

Shortest and Longest E-Mail Response Times

The 10 online companies with the quickest average e-mail response times are:

Rank	Company	Time
1.	OfficeDepot.com	48 minutes
2.	MusiciansFriend.com	58 minutes, 40 seconds
3.	Diapers.com	01:23:48
4.	DisneyStore.com	01:47:40
5.	Abercrombie.com	01:50:45
6.	USAutoParts.net	03:38:00
7.	Gilt.com	04:43:00
8.	PCMall.com	04:49:48
9.	Kohls.com	05:02.00
10.	Coldwatercreek.com	05:06:10

The 10 companies with the slowest average e-mail response times are:

Rank	Company	Time
1.	crateandbarrel.com	88:30:24
2.	Fingerhut.com	79:29:30
3.	Dell.com	65:10:45
4.	SwissColony.com	52:29:15
5.	MarketAmerica.com	39:35:36
6.	GreenMountainCoffee.com	39:20:12
7.	BestBuy.com	39:03:30
8.	Nike.com	37:17:36
9.	NorthernTool.com	35:45:50
10.	Williams-Sonoma.com	31:18:10

Elements of a Winning Style

If you're trying to persuade a company to offer a refund on a defective product or an exchange on an out-of-warranty product—if it's going to cost *them* money to make *you* happy—then you're headed uphill. Many companies hire skilled writers who have 1001 ways to persuade you to surrender.

There are some ways to get through these formidable walls. Here is what you should put into every complaint letter:

- *Solid as a rock research.* You'd be amazed—or really should not at this point—what you can find with a quick net search: everything from successful letters to the form replies they generated to tips for writing a letter. I started a wiki (www.onyoursi.de/wiki) with reader tips on sharing advice for successful grievance results. This is one place to begin. Not only does it help you know how to approach your problem, but it also helps set expectations.
- *Keep it tight.* The most effective e-mails and letters are unbelievably short—no more than three paragraphs or 175 words.

They include all the details necessary to track your problem, such as a receipt or an electronic confirmation. Remember, that's a real person on the other end trying to get to the point, so if you write something that goes on forever, it's possible they won't make it all the way to the end. (That's a good rule anyway; as Mark Twain is thought to have muttered: "If I'd had more time I'd have written less.")

■ *Being polite as rain.* Manners *really* matter. Customer service agents tell me time and again that cordial and grammatically correct missives catch their attention and make them want to offer better service. On the other hand, letters that are packed with four-letter words, threats, and ALL UPPERCASE receive the bare minimum in the way of responses—or nothing at all.

■ *Citing rules of the road.* Your complaint has the best chance of getting a fair shake if you can convince the company that it didn't follow its own rules or that it somehow broke the law. Usually you can find a copy of an end-user licensing agreement right in the box; however, sometimes the rules are less obvious. Your airline ticket rules aren't on your ticket, but in an almost unreadable document called the contract of carriage. If you have questions, ask the company for a copy of the contract or look on its site.

■ *Tell them what you want—use your sweet voice!* I've already mentioned the importance of a positive attitude. Be extra nice. Leaving this detail out could doom your request to failure. It leaves the question of "How do you fix this?" up to the customer-service representative—and rest assured, their answer will disappoint you more often than not.

■ *Copy every little one.* Yes, customer-service representatives review the list of everyone you copied on an e-mail or letter. When they see you've shared a grievance with a few other folks, it will give the complaint more weight. The people you copy will depend on the type of grievance. Just think of it as the exclamation mark at the end of your letter. You might want to let the government regulatory agency responsible know about the problem. Or, you may want to send it to a consumer advocate like me.

A concise, polite, well-researched, and targeted e-mail that specifically says how a company can address your grievance has the best chance of success. A rambling, vague, and overly emotional one is likely to never get answered, and in your heart you know nobody will read it.

But you can do everything right and still get turned down. I'll show you how to make sure that *doesn't* happen in the next chapter.

14

Turning a *No* into a *Yes*

To convert somebody go and take them by the hand and guide them.
—Thomas Aquinas

THERE'S NO WORSE feeling than knowing that a company took your worked-for money, gave you a shoddy product, and has no intention of ever returning the cash. And whenever I think of pig-headed, arbitrary corporate intransigence, I'm reminded of Scarlett.

Scarlett was the adorable baby African Gray parrot that my family bought from a pet store in the Florida Keys in 1995. Why was a struggling freelance writer shelling out $900 for an exotic bird? Beats me! The only thing dumber than that was shopping for the lowest price. If you want to buy an African Gray, you buy one from a reputable pet store, and your first concern should not be whether you pay $800 or $1,200 for it, but whether or not the bird is worth the price. It's a little like shopping for a car: Would you rather shell out $15,000 for a wheezing six-year-old Toyota with 120,000 miles on its odometer or $24,000 for a 2011 Ford Escort with all the bells and whistles?

I had some misgivings about the purchase. Scarlett looked frail, but the pet-store owner assured me she was just young, and that's what young parrots are *supposed* to look like. Though she was small

155

and scrawny, Scarlett and I quickly bonded. She perched on my knee and ruffled her feathers while I fed her. She squawked whenever I walked past her cage. African Grays are known for their intelligence and talkativeness. I looked forward to spending many years with my new friend. Then, just a few days after she came home with us, Scarlett fell to the floor of her cage one morning. As I cradled the baby bird in my hands, she breathed her last breath. I was completely despondent. A necropsy (that is, an autopsy performed on an animal) found that she'd had pneumonia, probably before we picked her up from the pet store.

In retrospect, it had all the makings of a Monty Python skit ("I'll tell you what's wrong with it, it's *dead*, that's what's wrong with it"), but I can tell you that returning her body to the pet store was the longest drive of my life. The pet-store owner took the bird and the cage and even after the necropsy results, offered me nothing. Not even a refund on the cage. Every effort to reason with her failed.

"You killed the bird," she said, jabbing an accusatory finger at me.

"That's not what the necropsy said," I replied.

"Yes, you did!"

"Did *not!*"

Around and around we went in circles. I felt foolish, resorting to childhood taunts. But the fact remained: She still had my $900.

Or did she? I had paid by credit card, and when negotiations with her collapsed, I phoned my bank and initiated a dispute. Even though my financial institution had a policy against contesting purchases of live animals, it made an exception for me after I provided ample evidence that my adversary had sold me a sick bird and kept every penny—including the cage I'd returned. I got every penny back.

Poor Scarlett's sad fate took me on a career turn. Winning my dispute showed me that consumers can fight back—and win, even when they think they have scant chance of gaining the upper hand. They just have to give it a shot.

You're Right

Part of the problem with today's customers is they believe they're getting what they paid for. The car that keeps breaking down? The

> **The Silent Majority by the Numbers**
>
> 96 percent: Number of dissatisfied customers who don't complain
>
> 63 percent: Silent dissatisfied customers who will not buy from a company again
>
> 15 percent: Customers who switch product brands because the company did not handle their complaint to their satisfaction

subprime mortgage you can no longer afford? The smartphone that makes you feel dumb? Thanks to call centers and customer service departments that send out form letters and employ operators who read scripted responses, you believe you *deserve* this. But you don't.

The customer may not always be *right*. But the customer has a *right* to be happy with a purchase. And that's true whether you're the victim of a traditional scam or business practices that take advantage more subtly. Developing an awareness of the corporate spin and the complacency that affects your attitude is a good place to start. But beyond that, you have to know that the system is stacked against you, and that you're actually right. It's your money, and you deserve to be satisfied with your purchase.

Why don't more people stand up for their basic rights? We've been conditioned to expect less. Most folks are made to feel they're asking too much—we are all basically polite people. A lot of us dislike confrontations. Sometimes it's a simple fact of believing these nasty, untrue words: "We've done as much as we can. We can offer you no more at this time."

You think?

How to Turn a *No* Around

When a company turns you down, you don't have to take their first no—or even their second or third. Here's how to appeal a rejection in writing.

Saying No before They Can

There's an *unwritten* rule that a book about consumer advocacy, and especially one that helps uncover grossly indecent scams, needs a final list of resources for people to go further on their own. The idea behind it is it enables readers (and participants in the positive future of consumerism) to find—and, I hope, avoid—disreputable businesses. I don't want to disappoint you, but keep in mind that everything can be manipulated, and even illegally, including the sites that rate businesses.

- *The American Customer Satisfaction Index* (http://www .theacsi.org) rates large companies and assigns them a score from 1 to 100. This is one of the most reliable ways of telling the legit status of a company.
- *Better Business Bureau* (http://bbb.org) "grades" businesses based on consumer complaints. A good grade can mean it's okay, but not a sure thing. However, BBB rankings can be shaped by clever corporations.
- *Consumer Reports* (http://consumersunion.org) is known primarily for its product ratings. But as I've outlined previously, it's far from perfect. It can point to a problematic company or product and remains among the most highly respected by consumers.
- *Epinions* (http://www.epinions.com) offers user-generated product reviews. But like all user review sites, it will attract malcontents (who all share the name Anonymous) who have had bad experiences with a product or service. What you see may not be an accurate representation.
- *JD Power* (http://www.jdpower.com) also rates products and companies, but like others I wouldn't rely on its ratings exclusively, as they tend to be vague and corporation-friendly.

- *Start at the bottom.* Give the system a chance to work. If you haven't already done so, contact the company through its customer service department. The point of this approach is to collect evidence that you gave the company an opportunity to make things right. This could be important later if the company tries to blow you off and you need to go to court.

- *Get a rejection in writing.* Don't accept no for an answer by phone; instead, ask the company to put it into an e-mail or letter. This gives you something to add to your file. Of course, I hope you won't be rejected; but if you are, you want cold, hard proof that the company gave you a thumbs-down. No worries; you're not out of options. In fact, you're just getting started.

- *Be patient.* The typical grievance takes six to eight weeks to resolve, in my experience. Yes, six to eight weeks. A lot of companies will get back to you sooner, but many routinely test the eight-week limit. There's no excuse for dragging things out, of course, but you must have patience when dealing with large companies— since they will almost certainly always test yours.

- *Appeal to a higher authority.* Did you get a form letter politely asking you to take a hike? Don't worry; it's still not over. Every company has a vice president of customer service or a manager who is in charge of dealing with the "customer experience"—and that's who needs to hear from you next. These executives go to great lengths to keep their names and contact information from becoming public. But a quick online search will reveal who they are and how to get in touch with them. I list many of them on my site, On Your Side (http://www.onyoursi.de).

- *Take another deep breath.* Don't overreact. Simply enclose copies of all the correspondence with a cover letter to the VP, politely asking the company to reconsider its decision. Copy the same group of people. Be pleasant and nonthreatening, but firm.

- *Take extreme measures.* If the company still says no, you should consider the Hail Mary approach—that is, overnighting a respectful but insistent letter directly to the chief executive officer along with the disappointing string of no's you've received. This is a little-known loophole in the system: something FedEx'ed to the top exec has an excellent chance of being read by that person. (That assumes the CEO has a high school diploma and is literate.)

- *Tell on 'em.* Contact law enforcement or regulatory authorities and ask them to investigate your complaint. A grievance to your state's insurance commission, local ombudsman, or to the Federal Trade Commission can have a truly magical effect.

- *Dispute the charge on your credit card.* This works more often than you'd think. If you believe you have a reasonable case, and the company refuses to entertain your request for a refund or a replacement, you may have no other choice than to dispute the purchase. Your rights under U.S. law are spelled out in the Fair Credit Billing Act; however, not all disputes are covered. And you'll want to read up on the law before invoking it (see box).

- *Go to court.* Most consumer complaints would be handled by a small-claims court, which doesn't require that you hire a lawyer. Companies like going to court about as much as the average person does, so filing a suit may be enough to get them to see things your way. Occasionally, the company won't send a lawyer to represent it and will simply default—in which case, you win.

- *Go to war.* In an age of blogging and social networking, there's one final court to which you can take your grievance: the court of public opinion. Starting a gripe blog can be therapeutic and can inflict untold damage on an intransigent company in the form of lost business. You should only consider this to be a last resort, since a gripe-site is a time-consuming and emotionally draining project. At the same time, it can be very rewarding.

Fair Credit Billing Act Basics

This 1975 law protects consumers from unfair billing practices and erroneous charges to their credit card. Federal law limits your responsibility for unauthorized charges to $50 and covers the following:

- Charges that list the wrong date or amount
- Charges for goods and services you didn't accept or weren't delivered as agreed
- Math errors
- Failure to post payments and other credits, such as returns

- Failure to send bills to your current address, with certain provisions
- Charges for which you request an explanation or written proof of purchase along with a claimed error or request for clarification

A Few Thoughts on the Art of Persuasion

I've seen my share of successful grievances, as well as a number of failed attempts. The ones that work are succinct, polite, and reasonable, and—perhaps most important—strike most people as reasonable. The ones that don't work have a few things in common:

- *They are too long.* The lengthier the missive, the less its chances of success. Think like a minimalist; offer only the information they'll need to consider your request. Remember, your letter should be no longer than a single page.
- *They are laundry lists of offenses that come across as whining.* Zero in on the main point and chuck the side grievances, like a customer service representative who showed disrespect. Nobody will care about that (they should, but they really don't). You need to make the case that you were ripped off, not slighted by some nobody.
- *They are exercises in hysteria.* Failed appeals for justice are often loaded with ventings that are beside the point. For example, claiming a company has ruined your life when it did no such thing, or threatening to sue the company for some trifling discourtesy will get you nowhere. Only a deadpan account of how you got ripped off, and an equally dispassionate threat to call the company to account, will set the offender to thinking: Whoops! This guy means business. Best to build bridges in this particular case.
- *They lack hard evidence of the company's wrongdoing.* Don't leave out any pertinent information even if it isn't in your favor. Acknowledge the case against you—then explain why it lacks validity. If you don't keep to this moral high ground, the company will write you off, not unjustifiably, as a liar.

- *They are empty threats.* Claiming that "I'll NEVER buy another product from your business again" always falls on deaf ears. To a 20-something who has other ideas about her career path, dismissing blowhards holds no risk to her low-level status in her company, and in fact might enhance it. (And speaking of lawsuits, threatening to take a company to court usually gets a case kicked to the legal department, where it may languish indefinitely. You don't want to go there unless you really mean it and have the financial wherewithal to carry out the threat. Admit it: You don't and won't.)

Do You Have a Case?

I often have the difficult task of telling people that they're wrong, and the company is right. You broke it, you pay. The TV is out of warranty. The terms on your contract are clear.

It might sound like an easy thing to do, but it's not. How do you let readers down gently without making them even *more* upset? Early on, my approach was to give it to them straight, by simply telling them that I was sorry but I couldn't mediate their case. That angered some readers to the point that they canceled their subscriptions to my newspaper. So I adopted a favorite tactic of corporate America—the stall. "Let me review this, and I'll be in touch if it's something I can help with." That's just another way of saying, "no, thank you."

But since you're reading this book, you deserve a straight answer. How do you figure out if your case has any merit? Here are a few questions to ask.

- *Did it get more than one rejection?* That can mean it's a weak case or you're making an unreasonable demand, and that it's time to ask more questions.
- *Do your friends or family think you're being reasonable?* Asking a trusted friend or associate to weigh in on the merits of your case may be a prudent move.

- *Can you find examples of others who have had similar problems?* If so, did the company handle their requests differently? If they were also rejected, chances are the company's refusal will stick.
- *Do you just feel like sticking it to 'em?* It's not that companies don't occasionally deserve a little payback, but if revenge is your only motive, your judgment may be clouded by emotion.

Sue or Shame?

As I've already mentioned, your two final options when you're not getting your way are going to a court of law or a court of public opinion. Both can be highly effective; both can also backfire.

A few years ago, several of my readers were snookered by an unlicensed insurance scam. The perpetrator was a modern-day snake-oil salesman who slithered from state to state, setting up shop and then pulling up his stakes and crossing state lines when authorities began closing in. He sold tens of millions of dollars' worth of fake travel protection policies through a network of travel agencies that asked few questions and cashed his generous commission checks. Finally a group of former customers caught up with him, I started writing about him on my blog, and the whole thing unraveled.

The customers threatened to sue anyone who was involved in the scheme, from travel agencies to the company that processed the transaction. They also took their campaign to the Internet, peppering my blog comments with threats. Much to their surprise, one of the travel agencies struck back quickly, filing a lawsuit against one of the group's leaders—and against *me* in apparent retaliation for covering the story.

Point is, you're playing in a different league when you start a hate-blog and throw around terms like *sue*—and you might not like the outcome of your actions. Then again, things could turn out just fine. The complaint against me went absolutely nowhere—it was what's known as a strategic lawsuit against public participation

(SLAPP)—designed to shut me up. But I had a good lawyer, and our strategy was to turn up the heat until the plaintiff phoned me on a Sunday afternoon, asking me what he had to do to make this go away.

- *The case for a gripe site.* Over the years, I've known many customers who built sites dedicated to their negative customer service experience or who created viral videos that inflicted millions of dollars of damage on a company's bottom line. Whether you choose to take your war to Twitter, Facebook, a blog, or YouTube, you must first believe that there is no other way, short of a lawsuit, to get what you want. Going public is a campaign of last resort and you have to be cautious.

   There's a right way and a wrong way to take a campaign to the Internet. I remember one disgruntled Expedia customer back in 2006 who had an airline ticket problem. This individual initiated a slash-and-burn online campaign with a flashy, overly emotional page that included ALL UPPERCASE descriptions of what happened. Sample: "I WAS ABANDONED IN EUROPE BY EXPEDIA AFTER THEY FAILED TO PROVIDE ME A TICKET I HAD ALREADY PAID WITH MY CREDIT CARD." (When I informed him after he contacted me that I was unable to help him to his satisfaction, he started e-mailing my editors and demanding my resignation. That only made him look crazier.) It's little wonder the online travel agency gave him the cold shoulder. Worse, disgruntled consumers who go off on their targets can sometimes lapse into libel and end up getting sued.

   I've also seen online campaigns that were successful in their attempts. One recent effort that comes to mind involved a guest at a Choice Hotel property involving its best-rate guarantee. After the hotel dismissed his request to have a price honored, he posted his correspondence between the hotel and himself online. It was rational, level-headed, and factual—and it caused the hotel chain to quickly reverse its decision.

- *The case for a lawsuit.* My experience with lawsuits has been similar to what I've found with online campaigns. Judges have a way of ferreting out frivolous, emotional lawsuits—if they ever make it in front of the court. A vast majority of consumer lawsuits end up in small claims court, where individuals can represent themselves. I personally know many aggrieved customers who showed up in small claims court with little preparation, a few receipts, and a lot of determination. And they won, even against trained attorneys.

Although I'm not a lawyer, I can say with some certainty that once you get beyond small claims and are playing in the big leagues, companies pay close attention to what you do. They'll send a lawyer, or even a team of lawyers instead of defaulting. They will prepare for the case. In fact, it's likely you'll face depositions and subpoenas long before your case goes to court, and the paperwork requirements alone may be enough to make you reconsider your case. The costs, both in time and money, may outweigh the benefits of a legal complaint.

■ *Beware of litigious companies.* Companies routinely threaten me with lawsuits. It simply comes with the territory of my profession. In fact, I probably wouldn't be doing my job as a consumer advocate to the best of my ability if corporate America completely approved of my actions. But companies who threaten customers are a far more serious thing—and believe me, they're out there. My advice? Before engaging in any social-media campaign or filing a lawsuit, do a simple search for the company name + "lawsuit" on your favorite search engine. Scroll down and go a few screens deep so that you can avoid search engine-optimized placements. If you see what appears to be a pattern; that is, if it looks like the company with which you're involved is overly litigious, you may want to switch from a lawsuit to an Internet campaign, or vice versa. By the way, ethical businesses with quality products only use the court system as a last resort. So a pattern may also be indicative of a sleazy company.

By the time you get to this point in a service dispute with the company, it's no longer a question of who's right and who's wrong; it's just about who has the best strategy. And that should be you.

Getting your way means that you must first come to the realization that you deserve to have your way. It means spinning a persuasive argument and not taking that inevitable first—or second, or third—no for an answer. It means realistically assessing your options and then acting on them fearlessly.

Ideally, though, you'd want to avoid all of that. And there *is* a way to do so.

15

Act Now

There's no time like the present.

—English proverb

IT'S STILL DARK outside when I tiptoe into my home office every morning, hoping not to wake my kids. My computer monitor flickers to life, illuminating a screenful of e-mails from readers. Almost all of them want the same thing: to be rescued.

There's one from an airline passenger describing the indignities she suffered on a recent flight in painstaking detail, complete with surly flight attendants, missed connections and, of course, a "ruined" vacation. A few days after coming home, she fired off a lengthy missive to the airline's CEO, and is upset that she hasn't heard back. "I need your help," she says.

There's another message from someone with a car problem. He's weary of leaving countless voice mail messages with his dealership, all of which have gone unanswered. "Would you contact them for me?" he asks. But I can see why they're ignoring him: His mother forgot to teach him manners. Who wants to respond to an expletive-filled message?

And there's another note from a woman who is three years into a dispute with her lawyer. Same problem—the attorney has gone into

167

radio silence. I read the e-mail chain. No wonder she's being ignored; her shrill demands make her look as if she's lost her grip on reality. She is what we in the biz refer to as a *gimme pig*.

On days like this, I ask myself: Why did you wait so long to do something? Why didn't you act sooner? And why are you relying on a third party to set things straight? Get crackin'. *You* are in charge of your life!

But then I remember that only a few years ago, I might have done *exactly* the same thing. I was the sucker who got bad service. I was scammed. All I could really do was throw a tantrum and ask anyone who would listen to me for help.

Whether you're eating a restaurant meal, staying at a hotel, or buying a loaf of bread at the grocery store, identifying a problem at the point of purchase makes a successful resolution far more likely than grumbling about it after the fact. In fact, armchair quarterbacking can make you the bad guy. Think about it. How can a business set things straight if you aren't around? How can it replace the meal you didn't like or provide a room discount if you aren't on the scene to accept its largesse?

But the act-now approach doesn't just apply to resolving problems. We begin to realize as we look at ways to fix the sick relationship between customers and companies that there's no time to waste. We have to do something—right *now*.

There's no time like the present to say "enough!" and let companies know that we're not going to take it anymore. And there's no time like the present to hold a mirror in front of your own face—and take a hard look at your habits as a customer.

Confession Time

Throughout this book, I've bared my soul about the many mistakes I've made as both a consumer and as a journalist. Why would I embarrass myself like that? Why not write this the way other books about consumerism have been framed, where the advocate *always* wins and looks like a superhero? Because that's not how life is. I've screwed up, and I'm not afraid to say it.

Fortunately, there's a lot to be learned from failure. Check out Kathryn Schulz's excellent book, *Being Wrong: Adventures in the Margin of Error*, for more on the upside of screwing up. I want you to feel comfortable admitting to your own shortcomings as a consumer. (I figured that if I go first, you won't mind doing it, either.) But more importantly, if we don't openly talk about our own defects, we'll never be able to avoid the schemes, swindles, and shady deals that await us out there.

Timing Is Everything

As someone who watches the ebb and flow between customers and companies every waking hour, I can confirm that time *isn't* on your side, regardless of your age. Companies benefit from delay far more than you ever could. Letting the clock run down is a time-honored trick—because before long, the statute of limitations has expired and you can't sue the company. Or—and this is more often the case—you just become so exasperated with a service problem that you walk away in disgust.

Companies hope you'll shrug off a problem without taking action. For example, the Federal Trade Commission's "cooling off" rule states that you can cancel a sale on certain items you purchased in your home—but you only have until midnight of the third business day after the sale. After that, like it or not, the product is yours. And that is fair enough. Do you think you should have a year to mull it over? Leveling the playing field means just that: You make yourself the equal of your corporate adversaries, not their master.

A lot of companies create customer service departments for what appear to be the sole purpose of stringing you along. They take their time answering grievances, either sending customer calls to an off-shore center where every question you ask is repeated *ad nauseam* by someone with a poor command of English. Or they send you an immediate form response that's followed by weeks of waiting. The last thing these organizations want is for their customers to take immediate and decisive action. Rather, they appear to want to draw the entire process out as much as possible.

Where's the Pain?

Here's a list of the most common consumer complaints. How many of these could have been resolved if action had been taken at the point of sale?

- *Auto.* Misrepresentations in advertising or sales of new and used cars, lemons, faulty repairs, leasing, and towing disputes.
- *Credit/Debt.* Billing and fee disputes, mortgage-related fraud, credit repair, debt relief services, predatory lending, illegal or abusive debt collection tactics.
- *Home Improvement/Construction.* Shoddy work, failure to start or complete the job.
- *Utilities.* Service problems or billing disputes with phone, cable, satellite, Internet, electric, and gas services.
- *Retail Sales.* False advertising and other deceptive practices; defective merchandise; problems with rebates, coupons, gift cards and gift certificates, failure to deliver.
- *Services.* Misrepresentations, shoddy work, failure to have required licenses, failure to perform.
- *Internet Sales.* Misrepresentations or other deceptive practices, failure to deliver online purchases.
- *Household Goods.* Misrepresentations, failure to deliver, faulty repairs in connection with furniture or appliances.
- *Landlord/Tenant* (tie). Unhealthy or unsafe conditions, failure to make repairs or provide promised amenities, deposit and rent disputes, illegal eviction tactics.
- *Home Solicitations* (tie). Misrepresentations or failure to deliver in door-to-door, telemarketing, or mail solicitations; do-not-call violations.
- *Health Products/Services.* Misleading claims, unlicensed practitioners, failure to deliver.

Source: 2009 Consumer Complaint Survey Report.

How to Find Better Service

We live in an always-on world where you can stream videos to your smartphone. There's no excuse for waiting until you get home to pull up consumer reviews on a product you've already purchased. If you're unhappy with the service you're getting in a store, you can do something *right now*. I post many of the names of service managers in the Appendix and on my site On Your Side (www.onyoursi.de).

Fixing What's Wrong with Business

It's true that companies continue to develop new and amazingly clever ways of winning your business. They manipulate their reputations and play mind games with search engines. They weave unreadable contracts that favor their own positions. They mess with our minds by using subliminal marketing techniques. These activities—and countless others—bleed their customers of billions of dollars every year. But in order for their schemes to work, we must be convinced that nothing we do matters—indeed, that all of this is inevitable.

These companies also need you to believe that even if something can be done, it will be a slow and gradual process. But that's not true.

There are ways to short-circuit these processes right *now*—which is exactly the right time to do it.

First and foremost, being aware of a *managed reputation* should ratchet up your skepticism about the material you read on a company and its products. The information you see—whether it's on a website, in a periodical, or on the products themselves—is tainted by rep management; so don't believe everything you read. Find trustworthy sources—including friends, reliable blogs, and publications—and only accept their recommendations when the consensus determines that a product is worth buying.

The same skepticism should apply to online search results, where black-hatters ply their dark craft. Search Engine Optimization (SEO) allows big companies to manipulate what you see when you're looking for something on the Internet. Find information from several search engines instead of just limiting yourself to one. Dig several screens into the search results instead of relying only on what you see on the first page. Taking this approach will hand an important defeat to the SEO pros who are trying to drive traffic to their client.

And what about the *deceptions*, *half-truths*, and sometimes even *outright lies* that companies use to separate you from your money? You can actually spot a vast majority of these with the sniff-test before you've fallen prey to them. Do they seem too good to be true? Can mouthwash really protect you from bad breath for 24 hours? Is a jail-broken phone really broken, or is the company telling a tall tale to protect its profits? Is the real estate market overvalued? Even the other lies—which companies call spin—can be revealed with a little research and common sense.

Companies try to promote themselves everywhere, not just in traditional ads, but also through product placements and other *unconventional methods*. You can identify these, too, if you know what to look for. More specifically, you must look *everywhere*. Agent Fox Mulder in *The X-Files* said it best: Trust no one.

Similarly, the increasingly *onerous contracts* that companies force you to sign when you buy a product can only be stopped if you *read* the agreements—the entire agreement. And if you don't like it, and the company won't change it, then refuse to buy the product.

Companies that engage in these questionable activities don't just risk alienating you, their customer. Over the long term, a business that cuts corners and offers shoddy service is doomed to fail. That's the central tenet of Raul Pupo's 2010 book, *America's Customer Service Meltdown: Restoring Service Excellence in the Age of the Customer*, who warns that corporations fixated on the bottom line, and shortcuts taken to boost profits, are buying a one-way ticket to their eventual insolvency. Unless managers wake up to this fact and begin making customer service a key part of their business strategy by instilling a service ethic and allowing front-line agents to serve customers, the future for American corporations is bleak.

Fixing Ourselves

How did we let these businesses take their unscrupulous behavior so far—and get away with it for so long? Why do we consistently make bad decisions about the products we buy? Why do we fall for obvious schemes that are intended to keep us loyal to a company that doesn't return the sentiment? Why do we get lulled into comfortable walled gardens from which escape seems impossible? Why don't we demand better information to help enlighten ourselves and one another?

Have we really failed to be responsible consumers? And is there a way to change that? Unfortunately, the answer to the first question is yes; and again, the answer to the second is that if we are to change it, it must happen now.

Although I find the research that concludes consumers often make *irrational purchasing decisions* to be persuasive, I'm not entirely convinced that these ludicrous choices are *inevitable*. I believe that we as consumers *choose* to expose ourselves to the product displays and pitches that lead to bad purchasing decisions. Short-circuiting the vast subconscious mind is really as simple as avoiding situations in which that part of the mind can make a decision for you. Your un-conscious mind is adaptive. If you take the time and trouble to learn rather than assume, you can hone your scam radar and become a better shopper without having to spend hours on every purchase.

Also, decisions to shop within the safety of a walled garden are made with the conscious mind: "Let's go to the mall! Let's log on to the Apple store!" I can't accept the fact that we make the decisions to frequent these places based solely on instinct. We do so because the garden is convenient. But being a responsible consumer isn't always convenient; in fact, it almost never is. If you want easy, you'll pay a steep price.

Sure, these traps are easy to step into. Loyalty programs, which almost always benefit the company more than the customer, force you to confine your business to one company. This in turn often prompts you to overspend for products that are cheaper elsewhere. It takes courage to cut up your frequent flier and valued member cards *right now*; however, that may be the best way to prevent further losses.

The underlying issue is that we simply don't understand what it means to be a *responsible consumer*. We don't ask for *useful information* about consumer products, nor are we willing to support such con-sumer advocacy as a general rule. Accepting the fact that being a good customer is a *job*—and that doing this job properly requires that we amass actionable information—will lead you to another conclusion: that there's absolutely no time to waste. No one will benefit from failing to act.

Who Wins?

When consumers become wise to the scams that companies perpetrate, do businesses lose? Not necessarily. Companies may believe that they benefit from ignorant customers who they can easily manipulate—and in some instances, they may be correct. But in their attempt to maintain the status quo, they fail to see a bigger picture: the fact that enlightened, educated, activist consumers can be even *better* customers.

For example, a 2011 survey found British mobile phone customers overspend by £200 a year because they buy calling plans and features they don't need. If customers picked the correct plan, then the mobile phone companies would benefit because they would have to innovate by finding and offering services that their customers needed or wanted. Plus, some of that £200 would be spent elsewhere, which would help other deserving businesses.

Besides, the idea that there has to be a winner and a loser is as antiquated as the notion that the customer is always right. Companies and consumers need one another, particularly in an unsteady economy.

Anyway, no one is *always* right.

Epilogue
Power in Your Pocket

What lies in our power to do, it lies in our power not to do.

—Aristotle

CHANGE—REAL CHANGE—IS in your hands. I've done what I can do.

The solution to the crisis in consumerism I've described isn't to regulate businesses into submission. Companies are smart, and their lawyers will figure out a way around any rules that stand in their way. (That's not to say I'm against *all* regulation, but I advocate it only when it's absolutely necessary and provably effective.)

It isn't to wage a campaign against evil or cruel businesses, either. That would be too simplistic, and it wouldn't solve a thing. It also incorrectly assumes that in this conflict there can be a winner and a loser, when all we are asking is to give good service at a fair price.

The power to make change lies firmly in your pocket and on whatever is slung over your shoulder. It's in your billfold, wallet, and purse.

When you hand over a dollar bill or credit card, you're endorsing not only a business's products and services, but also its current practices. This is your voting power. Refusing to spend your hard-earned money sends the unmistakable message that the business is doing something wrong.

Nothing speaks louder than the absence of your dollars.

You don't believe me? Consider the sad, lonely fate of the W.T. Grant Stores. The department store chain, which was founded in 1906, quickly rose to become the dominant retailer in U.S. urban centers. But as its customers migrated to the suburbs in the 1960s, the 1,200-store chain fell on hard times. Instead of adapting, it stood firm, insisting its customers would return if properly incentivized. In a bold but foolish move, W.T. Grant offered store credit to "anyone that breathed." It didn't work. The company went under in 1976 with the second-largest bankruptcy filing in U.S. history.

The lesson then was as it always is: Money talks. Take yours to a business that you know in your heart deserves it. This may mean that you have to drive a little farther out of your way or spend a little more on a competitor. And while you're at it, why not let your friends know about your disappointing experience, including all of your Facebook, Google+, and Twitter buddies? That'll hammer home the point that a business can't continue deceiving, manipulating, and offering substandard service. The business will get the message, and it *will* stop— or perish.

(And I beg you to recall the *good* purchases and share those just as boldly; why not reward the ones who do it best? It's a better Facebook status update than the grilled cheese sandwich you ate.)

However, until you stop being complicit in these schemes, swindles, and shady deals—until you say enough is enough—the scams in this book won't merely endure; they'll expand like a lopsided lizard in a badly directed horror flick.

Sidestepping the amateurs has been proven to be pretty easy. A little common sense and a lot of research are usually enough to ensure you won't get taken by a bad contractor or an unscrupulous innkeeper. The uppercase scams require a little more thought and strategy.

I'm thinking of the American airline industry, and especially the so-called legacy carriers that existed prior to government deregulation. US Airways is a company that routinely fails to deliver even the most basic customer service. It was the third most complained about airline in 2010, with a total of 795 grievances filed with the government (that's about $1\frac{1}{2}$ complaints filed per 100,000 passengers). Bear in mind, that number represents only a fraction of the actual complaints. That same year, the airline wouldn't have turned a profit without charging extra fees that its customers hate, nickeling and diming them for everything from a first checked bag to a ticket change fee.

And yet tens of thousands of air travelers book US Airways tickets every day. Why? Because the fares appear to be inexpensive and because its passengers see dollars, not service, when they make a reservation. They believe an airline ticket is an airline ticket, and most of all, they believe in a bargain. This mind-set has given rise to other bottom-feeding, customer-hostile air carriers, most notably the highly profitable Irish airline, Ryanair.

Do these companies deserve your money? No freaking way.

We can change that together. And I'm confident we will. The power is in you.

How to Connect with Me (and by *Connect* I Mean Talk to Me, Ask Me Questions, and Give Me Advice)

E-mail: elliottc@gmail.com

Blog address: (www.elliott.org or www.onyoursi.de)

Facebook: www.facebook.com/ChristopherJamesElliott

Foursquare: https://foursquare.com/elliottdotorg

FriendFeed: http://friendfeed.com/elliottdotorg

Google: https://profiles.google.com/elliottc

Google+: www.gplus.to/elliottdotorg

LinkedIn: www.linkedin.com/in/christopherelliott

Tumblr: http://elliottdotorg.tumblr.com/

Twitter: http://twitter.com/elliottdotorg

Appendix

Who You Gonna Call?

The Better Business Bureau

Although the Better Business Bureau is primarily an organization that serves corporations, a BBB complaint can force an unscrupulous business to respond to your grievance. Note that the BBB is divided into regions, so you will be referred to a BBB in your area.

> The Council of Better Business Bureaus
> 4200 Wilson Blvd, Suite 800
> Arlington, VA 22203-1838
> (703) 276-0100
> Complaint form: http://www.bbb.org/about/contactus.aspx

Consumer Financial Protection Bureau

The CFPB's mission is to make markets for consumer financial products and services work for Americans. It supervises banks, credit unions, and other financial companies, and ensures federal consumer financial laws are enforced. As a relatively new agency, however, its effectiveness has yet to be tested. The most effective way to file a complaint is online: http://www.consumerfinance.gov/get-help-now/consumer-questions-and-complaints/.

1801 L Street, NW
Washington, DC 20036
1(855)-411-CFPB (2372)

Federal Trade Commission

The FTC doesn't resolve individual disputes, but a complaint to this federal agency can bring some pressure to bear on an ethically challenged company.

600 Pennsylvania Avenue, NW
Washington, DC 20580
(202) 326-2222
www.ftc.gov
Toll-free helpline: 1-877-FTC-HELP (1-877-382-4357)
Complaint form: www.ftccomplaintassistant.gov

National Association of Consumer Advocates

A national organization of more than 1,500 attorneys who represent and have represented hundreds of thousands of consumers victimized by fraudulent, abusive, and predatory business practices.

1730 Rhode Island Avenue, NW
Ste 710
Washington, DC 20036
(202) 452-1989
Contact form: www.naca.net/contact-us

Your State's Attorney General

As chief legal officers of the states, commonwealths, and territories of the United States, the attorney general serves as counselor to state government agencies and legislatures, and as representatives of the public interest. You can find your state's AG at the National Association of Attorneys General website, www.naag.org/.

How to Find a Manager in Person

The best way to fight bad service is right now, in real time. Don't wait to get home. Businesses expect you to put it off, so by the time you've written a letter or figured out what to say by phone, you can bet the company has prepared an appropriate response.

Say something. Now.

Not always easy, I know. You have to take a deep breath and speak up and be prepared to stand your ground. But it's by and large the fastest way to get a resolution.

Why?

- A company has more ways to make you happy when you're disappointed with a product. They can exchange it, fix it, or offer you a refund on the spot.
- Employees and their supervisors are also allowed to offer these extras to their customers, so they can ensure you walk away happy. It's not that easy when you're doing it by phone or e-mail.
- The appeals process is usually pretty simple. Just ask for a manager, who is usually more than happy to listen to your case and can bend even more rules to make you whole.

The process usually goes like this: Something bad happens, and you mention it to an employee. If the employee can't fix the problem, you ask for a supervisor, until it gets taken care of.

But what if it isn't? What if the employee you're dealing with is dismissive? And what if that person refuses to call a manager or claims no one is available?

I've been in that situation before. Maybe it was my own attitude (after all, when you're upset at the level of service, it's hard to hide your feelings of disappointment) or maybe it was the business. I've stormed out of my share of businesses when I should have stood my ground.

Here's what you should do instead.

- *Take a deep breath.* You're probably upset. That's the last thing you want when you're negotiating. If you're in the grip of a powerful emotion like anger, you aren't thinking clearly. So, if need be, find a quiet corner and calm yourself.
- *Look around.* The picture and name of a supervisor is often posted on the wall. It's not always in a prominent place. (Hint: check the hallways leading to the back offices or the bathrooms.) From that point, it's just a matter of requesting that person by name.

■ *Mind your manners.* Remain unflappable and nonargumentative and use lots of "pleases" and "thank yous." Allow the shoddy product or service to speak for itself. For example, a server is likely to be outraged by an insect baked into your restaurant meal, so there's no need to add your own drama to it. And there's never a reason—ever—to be rude. A manager is far likelier to show up when a customer is behaving rationally.

■ *Ask for more information.* Assuming an employee can't help, you can underscore your seriousness by politely asking for a manager's contact information, including a name, phone number, and mailing address. That signals to the employee that you're not simply walking away. There's no need to add threats like, "You'll be hearing from my attorney!" Often, the simple request for information will prompt an employee to summon the boss.

■ *Praise them.* Another well-known technique for bringing a supervisor out into the store is with the promise of positive feedback. Tell an associate that you want to share something good with his supervisor; make sure you actually have something good to share. This often works like a charm, because everyone likes an "atta-boy." After lavishing your praise, note that there's one area of improvement you'd like to suggest, and then let 'em have it.

■ *Ask an unanswerable question.* If you stump the employee, they'll have to check with a supervisor. That often means the manager must come out to speak with you, to make sure your question is understood.

■ *Be supportive . . . and polite.* It's often true that employees don't have the power to make something right. That doesn't necessarily mean they're incompetent, just that they're not allowed to do anything. Employees are far likelier to call a manager if you can offer assurances that you won't disparage them. How? By explaining that you know it's not their fault that their hands are tied. And by being polite.

In a perfect world, you wouldn't have to call a manager. In a perfect world, the problem you're having wouldn't exist at all—you'd be getting the service you paid for.

It's not a perfect world.

How to Find a Manager by E-Mail

Knowing the right person can mean the difference between being ignored and getting the service you deserve. It's a sad fact that some e-mails never reach a company, while others are lost or are ignored.

Don't let that happen to you. Here are the steps to finding the right name and e-mail address.

- *Do a smart search online.* Major companies usually list the names of their executives on their websites. In your favorite search engine, just type "site: companyname.com," "e-mail," and "customer service manager" or "vice president." You can add the term "customer service" if you pull up too many results. That could reveal the name and e-mail address of the right person to contact. (The "site:" modifier ensures you're just searching the company website.)
- *Take an informed guess.* You may not find a working e-mail address, but it's not hard to guess it. You should assume managers won't carelessly post their e-mail address online (although you'd be surprised). That doesn't mean they don't have an e-mail address.

Guess who?

A former employee at Tiffany offers the following case study for how to guess a CEO's e-mail address: Let's say you have a problem with that silver bracelet you bought for your better half. Let's also assume that e-mails to the company are being ignored, which she assures me is unlikely.

Searching for e-mails at the @tiffany.com domain would reveal that all e-mails either follow the convention firstname .lastname@tiffany.com or firstname_lastname@tiffany.com. Finding the CEO's name is easy—just look up a list of its corporate executives online. I won't keep you in suspense: it's Michael Kowalski. Then try a few of the conventions, remembering that they sometimes also use a middle initial.

(continued)

> (*continued*)
> The correct e-mail address could be michaeljkowalski@tiffany.com or michael_kowalski@tiffany.com or michael.kowalski@tiffany.com—or some other variation.
> "So now I know the CEO's name, I will send him an e-mail trying a few of these," says the ex-employee.

- *Ask for help.* If you're looking for some expert assistance at finding the right contact without having to hire a private investigator, check out Amazon's Mechanical Turk (https://www.mturk.com/). It lets you post the equivalent of a "want" ad for information, and an army of researchers is at your command.
- *Verify the e-mail address.* There's a way to tell if the e-mails you've collected will work. A site called Free E-mail Verifier (http://verify-e-mail.org/) allows you to check an address. I recently had to update the name of a customer service contact at an airline after a previous manager left. The company wouldn't give me the name of the new manager, because they knew I would post his name and e-mail address on my customer service wiki. I found his name through an online search, made an educated guess about his e-mail address, and used Free E-mail Verifier to make sure it was accurate.

If you get a bounce back or two, don't worry. Keep trying. Sending an e-mail is free, and eventually you'll guess the correct address and connect with a manager who can help you.

Remember, these managers don't have the right to keep their e-mails private. They are there to serve you, and if the e-mail you sent to the company is being ignored, they need to hear from you.

How to Find a Manager by Phone

Getting the phone number for a company is easy: It's listed in every directory, and the company wants you to call it so it can sell you something.

Finding the direct extension of a customer service manager? That's not so easy.

Here's a true story: I was at a recent customer service conference, and after a friendly conversation with several managers, I offered my card. They didn't reciprocate, instead claiming they had "just run out."

Yeah, *right*.

They were afraid I'd publish their phone numbers online. (With good reason; I would have.)

Maybe it's just me, but you have the right to call the vice president of customer service or even the president of the company when his or her team fails to meet your expectations. You shouldn't have to wander aimlessly through the phone tree of a company, pressing zero in the hopes of being transferred to an offshore call center.

No, you deserve better than that. Here's how you can get a direct line.

- *Yes, the numbers are sometimes posted online.* They're sometimes firewalled on services like LinkedIn (www.linkedin.com) or Jigsaw.com (www.jigsaw.com), but it's easy to get in by signing up for a membership, which costs nothing.
- *Call after hours.* If you phone a company after business hours, you'll go straight to the company directory. You can dial the name of the customer service manager using your keypad and leave a message for that person. That's often the quickest way to alert a company to your problem, especially if it's an immediate one that can't be done through e-mail.
- *Zero is your friend.* If you find yourself getting bounced to an assistant's phone mail, don't worry. A lot of voice mail systems will assign another person to pick up if that person isn't there; just punch "0" before the beep, and you'll be transferred to that person.
- *Be polite.* Between 5 P.M. and 7 P.M., you can find a lot of people working late, even though the switchboard operators have gone home for the day. If they pick up, just be nice and say, "Oh, I was trying to reach so-and-so (insert name of manager). Do you know what his/her extension is?" Often, they'll give it to you for the asking (this is an old reporter trick, but it works great for anyone).

- *Two words: company directory.* A disgruntled former employee once mailed me the phone directory from her company. None of the information was proprietary, but it sure came in handy when customers asked for a phone number from that company. You'd be surprised where these company directories are left. Sometimes you can find one in the lobby of the business, unguarded. Channel your inner spy and use your cell phone to take snapshots of a few relevant pages.
- *Try an alternate number.* Oddly, some customer managers readily reveal their private phone numbers, and even their cell phone numbers, to groups that then post the information online. I've found these in college alumni directories and nonprofit organizations that list their donors online.
- *Phone home.* As a last-ditch effort—and I really do mean last in the ditch—try phoning a manager at home. Many homes still have landlines, and executives don't want to pay extra to keep the numbers unlisted. If you really need to get through, and all else has failed, go for it.

One more thing: Beware of free phone search scams. As I write this, there are several sites that charge you for running a search for personal information, like a cell phone number, address, and any other public records relating to the person. Don't fall for it. You can find all the information you need online or with a little sleuthing, at no extra cost, since many times the search services employ people who do what you'd do!

Of course it shouldn't be necessary to call a manager. The frontline employees at a company should take care of your question or concern quickly. But in the unlikely event that you have to go above their heads, these tried-and-true techniques will serve you well.

How to Find a Manager through Social Media

A phone call or e-mail may not be the best way of getting better customer service. Sometimes, social media like Facebook, Google+, Twitter, or, the latest favorite, LinkedIn, can do the trick.

A quick word about search. While many social networks are easily searchable through one of your favorite search engines, the sand shifts by the day.

One day Twitter may be searchable on Google; the next day, it might not. Ditto with Facebook and LinkedIn. It's all a matter of what the companys' boards decide—and these decisions are mercurial.

I've found the best way to search for something on the network is while you're on it (that's especially true for Facebook). But there are other ways to find your way around, including search engines like Followerwonk (www.followerwonk.com), or Twinitor (http://www .twinitor.com/) which search Twitter, and attending regular company "Tweetups," or offline meetings attended by executives.

Facebook

Everyone is on Facebook now, even your grandma. That includes companies and individuals—among them, numerous customer service managers and CEOs. Friending a manager may be tricky. If you're trying to contact someone for the express purpose of complaining, it might be difficult to persuade that person to accept your friend request. However, there are no such restrictions on a company page—and once you "like" a company, you're often free to post whatever you want on its wall. (Companies tend to hire specialists to watch their walls, so don't be surprised if the post is scrubbed and you're contacted by a representative.) However, I'm surprised how little is done to truly monitor these pages; when Target was the . . . target of slurs, after its nonprofit division donated money to an antigay organization, those nasty comments and posts stayed on the like page for weeks!

Google+

It's only a matter of time before this network becomes one of the first places customers go when they have a customer service problem. Every business will be there, as well as millions of customers. Google's business profiles are still emerging, but the way you can interact with other customers through video conferencing, chat, and its Circles format has already proven effective. It will become a powerful way to pressure a company to do the right thing, particularly if you have friends and they have friends. Finding individual managers through Google+ may be hard if they're not available through search, but the good news is that if you can't find a profile, it probably doesn't exist. Google in mid-2011 eliminated private profiles.

Twittering for Better Service

Barb Staigerwald got an unexpected e-mail one Saturday morning. Her hotel reservation in San Diego had been canceled without explanation. This wasn't just any hotel room; it was a weekend at the Hotel Solamar during a large convention. Replacing it would be impossible.

After getting nowhere by phone, she fired up her PC and found the president and chief operating officer of the hotel chain that owned the Solamar, Kimpton Hotels & Restaurants, on Twitter.

A few polite tweets to @Niki_Leondakis later, Staigerwald had her room back, and an apology for the inconvenience.

Twitter

For real-time resolutions of problems that can be solved through normal means such as asking a manager (i.e., someone who can make something happen) for help, Twitter excels. You don't have to follow anyone; just know the Twitter handle of the manager and the company. So, adding @Niki_Leondakis and @Kimpton Hotels to the end of Staigerwald's tweet would have been enough to get their attention. No need to establish a friendship, unless you want to send a direct message, in which you have to follow each other. Having a lot of followers can give your complaint some weight, but it's not absolutely essential. On Twitter, a call-out is an actual call-out, and good (or paranoid) companies pay attention to all of them.

LinkedIn

This is your secret weapon for better service because almost every business is on this network. Once you're on board, you can get "introduced" to anyone from a company by way of a mutual friend, and often you can ask for an introduction yourself. I find managers and CEOs on LinkedIn all the time, and approaching them is easy. There's an assumption that anybody on LinkedIn is a professional and wants to conduct business. Don't be the reason for someone to think otherwise.

These four social networks should be able to connect you quickly with a manager of any business.

Bibliography

Prologue

Federal Trade Commission Consumer Complaints, "FTC Releases List of Top Consumer Complaints in 2010; Identity Theft Tops the List Again," Federal Trade Commission, March 3, 2011, www.ftc.gov/opa/2011/03/topcomplaints .shtm/.

Introduction

Federal Trade Commission Consumer Complaints, "FTC Releases List of Top Consumer Complaints in 2010; Identity Theft Tops the List Again," Federal Trade Commission, March 3, 2011, www.ftc.gov/opa/2011/03/topcomplaints .shtm/.

Christopher Elliott, "Liar, Liar! 28 Percent of Hotel Guests Admit They Stretched the Truth for a Discount," *Consumer Traveler*, February 14, 2011, www.consumertraveler.com/today/liar-liar-28-percent-of-hotel-guests-admit-they-stretched-the-truth-for-a-discount/.

Kate Reynolds and Lloyd Harris, "When Service Failure Is Not Service Failure: An Exploration of the Forms and Motives of 'Illegitimate' Customer Complaining," *Journal of Services Marketing* 19, no. 5 (2005), www.emerald insight.com/journals.htm?articleid=1513536&show=pdf/.

"The Global Retail Theft Barometer," Centre for Retail Research (2010), www .globalretailtheftbarometer.com/.

Guy Winch, *The Squeaky Wheel: Get Results, Improve Your Relationships, Enhance Your Self-Esteem* (New York: Walker and Company, 2011).

P. Kumaraguru, S. Sheng, L. Acquisti, and J. Hong, "Teaching Johnny Not to Fall for Phish," ACM *Transactions on Internet Technology* 5, no. N. (2004), www.heinz.cmu.edu/~acquisti/papers/johnny_paper.pdf/.

A. Mokdad, J. Marks, D. Stroup, and J. Gerberding, "Actual Causes of Death in the United States, 2000," *Journal of the American Medical Association* 291, no. 10 (2004): 1238–1245, http://jama.ama-assn.org/content/291/10/1238.abstract/.

Theodore Malloch, *Doing Virtuous Business: The Remarkable Success of Spiritual Enterprise* (Nashville, TN: Encounter Books, 2008).

J. Damooei, "Emphasis on Teaching Ethics in Business Schools: The Recent Experiences in Higher Education" (2007), http://lass.calumet.purdue.edu/cca/jgcg/2007/fa07/jgcg-fa07-damooei.htm/.

M. Keenan and B. Sullivan, "Duke Probe Shows Failure of Post-Enron Ethics Classes," www.bloomberg.com/apps/news?pid=newsarchive&sid=aEL5ZnKhQuXY/.

Chapter 1

Sensibill.com, "Online Reputation Management and Web Design" (2010), www.braginteractive.com/wp-content/downloads/pdfs/Online-Reputation.pdf/.

Brag Interactive, "Brag Interactive's Mission" (2011), http://braginteractive.com/brag-interactives-mission/.

Mindsay Blog, "Defend Matrix Business: Protecting Online Brand" (2010), http://defendmatrix.mindsay.com/defend_matrix_protecting_your_reputation.mws/.

Michelle Leder, "Footnoted Blog" (2011), www.footnoted.com, written by Michelle Leder, author of the 2003 book, *Financial Fine Print: Uncovering a Company's True Value* (Hoboken, NJ: John Wiley & Sons).

Wendy Fried, "Rite-Aid, Revisited . . ." (2008), www.footnoted.com/odds-and-ends/rite-aid-revisited/.

Michelle Leder, "Taking Off at Northwest and Continental . . ." (2008), www.footnoted.com/my-big-fat-deal/taking-off-at-northwest-and-continental/.

Michelle Leder, "What Happens in Vegas . . ." (2009), www.footnoted.com/my-big-fat-deal/what-happens-in-vegas-2/.

John Mackey's Blog, "Whole Foods" (2008), www2.wholefoodsmarket.com/blogs/jmackey/2008/05/21/back-to-blogging/#more-26/.

Erik Rhey, "Corporate Sock Puppets," *PC Magazine*, September 12, 2007, www.pcmag.com/article2/0,2817,2182886,00.asp/.

Nick Fielding and Ian Cobain, "Revealed: US Spy Operation that Manipulates Social Media," (2011), www.guardian.co.uk/technology/2011/mar/17/us-spy-operation-social-network/.

"Survey: Companies Worry More About Reputational Risk," *Business Ethics* (August 2010), http://business-ethics.com/2010/08/10/1745-survey-companies-worry-more-about-reputational-risk/.

Christopher Elliott, "How Companies Bend the Truth Online: 5 Secrets Consumers Should Know," On Your Side, November 12, 2010, http://onyoursi.de/2010/11/how-companies-bend-the-truth-online-5-secrets-consumers-should-know/.

Gary Bahadur, *Privacy Defended: Protecting Yourself Online* (Que Publishers, Indianapolis, 2002).

Mark Cox, "85 Percent of Consumers Would Pay More for Exceptional Customer Experience," Crack, October 18, 2010, www.crackexp.com/blog/85-percent-of-consumers-would-pay-more-for-exceptional-customer-experience/.

Elliott, "How Companies Bend the Truth Online."

Bruce Schneier, "Schneier on Security," June 24, 2011, www.schneier.com/blog/archives/2011/06/selling_a_good.html.

Paul Marsden, Alain Samson, and Neville Upton, "Advocacy Drives Growth," *Brand Strategy* (2005), 45–47, www.scribd.com/doc/36324206/Advocacy-Drives-Growth/.

Elliott, "How Companies Bend the Truth Online."

Lisa Hankin, "The Effects of User Reviews on Online Purchasing Behavior Across Multiple Product Categories," University of California, Berkeley (2007), www.ischool.berkeley.edu/files/lhankin_report.pdf/.

Vince Veneziana, "Should IZEA Advertisements Be Accepted on TechCrunch?" (2007), http://techcrunch.com/2007/11/25/should-izea-advertisements-be-accepted-on-techcrunch/.

Seth Porges, "PayPerPost's Latest Gimmick—SocialSpark" (2007), http://techcrunch.com/2007/11/10/payperposts-latest-gimmick-socialspark/.

Temkin Group, "Top Ten Ratings for 2011" (2011), www.temkinratings.com/.

Terry Macalister, "BP's Deepwater Horizon Oil Spill Likely to Cost More than Exxon Valdez" (2010), www.guardian.co.uk/environment/2010/apr/30/bp-cost-deepwater-horizon-spill/.

"Broken Guitar Song Gets Airline's Attention," CBC News (2009), www.cbc.ca/news/arts/music/story/2009/07/08/united-breaks-guitars.html/.

Alex Alvarez, "On CNN, Combative GoDaddy CEO Explains Why He Killed An Elephant . . . And Will Again" (2011), www.mediaite.com/tv/on-cnn-combative-godaddy-ceo-explains-why-he-killed-an-elephant-and-will-again/.

Eric Snyder, "FTC Fines Legacy Learning Systems $250k for 'Misleading' Ads," *Nashville Business Journal*, March 18, 2011, www.bizjournals.com/nashville/news/2011/03/18/ftc-fines-legacy-learning-systems.html/.

Chapter 2

Daniel Ruby, "The Value of Google Result Positioning," Chitika Insights (2010), http://insights.chitika.com/2010/the-value-of-google-result-positioning/; and Optify, "Marketing in Real Time," www.optify.net/guides/organic-click-through-rate-curve/.

Christopher Elliott, "Can You Use Aggressive SEO—and Deliver Good Customer Service?" CBS interactive (2011), www.bnet.com/blog/customer-management/can-you-use-aggressive-seo-8211and-deliver-good-customer-service/101/.

Trend Metrix Software, "SEO Case Study: Canadian Florist Website," Search Engine Optimization (SEO) Case Studies and Customer Testimonials (2011), www.trendmx.com/seo-services/seo-services-case-study.aspx/.

Vanessa Fox, "New York Times Exposes JCPenney Link Scheme That Causes Plummeting Rankings in Google" (2011), http://searchengineland.com/new-york-times-exposes-j-c-penney-link-scheme-that-causes-plummeting-rankings-in-google-64529/.

Vanessa Fox, "Google's Action Against Paid Links Continues: Overstock and Forbes Latest Casualties; Conductor Exits Brokering Business" (2011), http://searchengineland.com/googles-action-against-link-schemes-continues-overstock-com-and-forbes-com-latest-casualties-conductor-exits-business-65926/.

Danny Sullivan, "Google's 'Gold Standard' Search Results Take Big Hit in *New York Times* Story" (2010), http://searchengineland.com/googles-gold-standard-results-take-hit-new-york-times-57081/; Danny Sullivan, "DecorMyEyes Merchant Vitaly Borker Arrested After *NYT* Piece on Google Rankings" (2010), http://searchengineland.com/decormyeyes-merchant-vitaly-borker-arrested-after-nyt-piece-on-google-57921/.

University of Michigan, "Airline Satisfaction Running on Empty: Airlines Skid into Last Place in The American Customer Satisfaction Index, while Fast Food and Hotels Serve Up More Satisfaction to Customers," www.theacsi.org/; and Dawn Anfuso, "Online Research Drives Offline Sales," The American Interactive Consumer Survey, conducted by The Dieringer Research Group (2004), www.imediaconnection.com/content/4355.imc/.

Karen Aho, "The Customer Service Hall of Shame," MSN Money (2010), http://articles.moneycentral.msn.com/Investing/Extra/the-customer-service-hall-of-shame-2010.aspx/.

U.S. Department of Transportation, "Air Travel Consumer Report," Aviation Consumer Protection and Enforcement (2011), http://aircon sumer.ost.dot .gov/reports/index.htm/.

Federal Trade Commission, "FTC Issues Report of 2009 Top Consumer Complaints" (2010), www.ftc.gov/opa/2010/02/2009fraud.shtm/.

Chapter 3

Dan Shapley, "Study: 98% of Products' Green Claims Are Misleading," Yahoo! Green (2009), http://green.yahoo.com/blog/daily_green_news/25/study-98-of-products-green-claims-are-misleading.html/.

Mitch Lipka, "Gotcha! When Companies Make False Claims," MSN Money (2011), http://money.msn.com/saving-money-tips/post.aspx?post=50be0368-55e1-46f2-9fbc-d9c69bc39602/.

Federal Trade Commission, "FTC Action Puts Deceptive Marketer Out of the Debt Relief Business" (2010), www.ftc.gov/opa/2010/12/creditdebt.shtm/.

Federal Trade Commission, "Deceptive Marketers Banned from Selling Mortgage Relief Services; One Defendant Ordered to Pay $11.5 Million" (2010), www.ftc.gov/opa/2010/07/lmshope.shtm/.

Federal Trade Commission, "FTC Settlement Prohibits Marketers of Children's Vitamins from Making Deceptive Health Claims about Brain and Eye Development" (2010), www.ftc.gov/opa/2010/12/nbty.shtm/.

Chris Morran, "FTC: Dannon Agrees to Stop Selling Activia as Cure for Irregularity," The Consumerist (2010), http://consumerist.com/2010/12/ftc-dannon-agrees-to-stop-selling-activia-as-cure-for-irregularity.html/.

"National Public Survey on White Collar Crime," National White Collar Crime Center (2010), www.nw3c.org/research/national_public_survey.cfm/.

Christopher Elliott, "Lying to Your Customers? Come on, Everyone's Doing It," CBS Interactive Business Network (2011), www.bnet.com/blog/management/lying-to-your-customers-come-on-everyones-doing-it/3889/.

Amy Novotney, "Beat the Cheat," *Monitor on Psychology* 42, no. 6 (June 2011), www.apa.org/monitor/2011/06/cheat.aspx/.

Jen Barth, "The Changing American Shopper," Kelton Research Study (2009), www.keltonresearch.com/study/recession/.

Christopher Elliott, "Honest Guest's Guide to Free Hotel Amenities" (2010), http://today.msnbc.msn.com/id/35840385/ns/today-todaytravel/t/honest-guests-guide-free-hotel-amenities/.

Peter Greenberg, "Guests Are Still Stealing Hotel Goods, (2007), www .hotelchatter.com/story/2007/5/22/114315/209/hotels/Guests_Are_Still_ Stealing_Hotel_Goods/.

Bob Sullivan, *Gotcha Capitalism: How Hidden Fees Rip You Off Every Day—And What You Can Do About It* (New York: Ballantine Books, 2007).

Laine Doss, "Wendy's Natural-Cut Fries Not So Natural After All," Broward Palm Beach New Times Blogs (2011), http://blogs.browardpalmbeach.com/cleanplatecharlie/2011/04/wendys_natural_cut_fries_not_s.php/.

Brad Foss, "FTC Finds Minimal Gas Price Gouging after Katrina," *Daily Herald*, May 22, 2006, www.heraldextra.com/business/article_918c8157-68f3-5488-a757-0245d70845d0.html/.

Christopher Elliott, "Your Products Are a Scam—Or Are They?" CBS Interactive, April 28, 2011, www.bnet.com/blog/customer-management/your-products-are-a-scam-8212-or-are-they/168/.

Health.org, "Fresh Breath for 12 Hours?" *Consumer Reports* (2008), www.consumerreports.org/health/healthy-living/news/2008/7/smartmouth-mouthwash/overview/smartmouth-mouthwash-ov.htm/.

Chapter 4

Dan Keller, "Another Way to Make Money on Twitter (and Blogging)," Tycoon Blogger (2010), http://tycoonblogger.com/monetize-your-blog/mylikes-another-way-to-make-money-on-twitter-and-blogging.

James Johnson, "Accepting Unknown Friends on Facebook Can Get Your Account Easily Hacked," The Blog Herald (2011), www.blogherald.com/2011/05/25/accepting-unknown-friends-on-facebook-can-get-your-account-easily-hacked/.

Christopher Elliott, "This Britney Spears Video Is an Ad—Can You Tell?" CBS Interactive (2011), www.bnet.com/blog/customer-management/thisbritney-spears-video-is-an-ad-1812-can-you-tell/174.

Christopher Elliott, "This Britney Spears Video Is an Ad—Can You Tell?" CBS Interactive (2011), www.bnet.com/blog/customer-management/this-britney-spears-video-is-an-ad-8212-can-you-tell/174.

J. Patel, M. Chesler, and H. Leung, "Deutsche Bank: Online media buyers survey—11% ad growth in 2011" (2011) www.dm2pro.com/downloads/20110119_1/download.

NielsenWire, "Global Advertising: Consumers Trust Real Friends and Virtual Strangers the Most" (2009), http://blog.nielsen.com/nielsenwire/consumer/global-advertising-consumers-trust-real-friends-and-virtual-strangers-the-most.

Thomas Claburn, "Half of Mobile Ads Clicked By Mistake," *Information Week*, January 28, 2011, www.informationweek.com/news/software/bi/229200047.

Andy Beal, "Forrester Predicts Huge Growth for Social Media Marketing," Marketing Pilgrim (2009), www.marketingpilgrim.com/2009/04/forrester-social-media-growth.html.

Erick Schonfeld "Industry Insiders Say Online Video Advertising Is Reaching a 'Frenzy Point'" (2010), http://techcrunch.com/2010/08/20/online-video-advertising-frenzy/.

The Cajun Boy, "Get Paid to Tweet, Facebook and Comment on Blogs. Facebook Post Ad" (2009), http://gawker.com/#!5253213/get-paid-to-tweet-facebook-and-comment-on-blogs (2009).

Christopher Elliot, "Advertising Reality Check: Are You Leading—or Lying?" CBSNews.com (May 6, 2011), www.cbsnews.com/8301-505125_162-49140204/advertising-reality-check-are-you-leading-or-lying.

Harry Weber, "AirTran to Sell Advertising on Seatback Tray Tables," *USA Today*, November 7, 2009, www.usatoday.com/travel/flights/2009-11-17-airtran-seatback-advertising_N.htm/.

Annys Shin, "FTC Moves to Unmask Word-of-Mouth Marketing," *Washington Post*, December 12, 2006, www.washingtonpost.com/wp-dyn/content/article/2006/12/11/AR2006121101389.html?nav=rss_technology.

Bernays anecdote from Wendell Potter, *Deadly Spin* (New York: Bloomsbury Press, 2010), 56.

Anita Lienert, "Buyers Feel Regret as Cash for Clunkers Final Tally Is Released," Edmunds Inside Line (2009), www.insideline.com/car-news/buyers-feel-regret-as-cash-for-clunkers-final-tally-is-released.html.

Chapter 5

AAA South, "Membership Terms and Conditions of Use" (2010), www.aaasouth.com/main_terms.aspx.

Lavasoft.com Spyware Statistics (2007), www.lavasoft.com/support/spyware educationcenter/spyware_statistics.php.

Peter Jennings, "Fine Print May Waive Legal Rights," abcNews/Money (2005), http://abcnews.go.com/Business/LegalCenter/story?id=522724&page=1 (2005); and Public Citizen, "The Arbitration Trap: How Credit Card Companies Ensnare Consumers," www.citizen.org/publications/publicationredirect.cfm?ID=7545; and "Stacked Deck: A Statistical Analysis of Forced Arbitration," Center for Responsible Lending (2009), www.responsiblelending.org/credit-cards/research-analysis/stacked-deck-a-statistical-analysis-of-forced-arbitration.html.

Forum selection clause, Wikipedia: The Free Encyclopedia (2011), http://www
.lacba.org/showpage.cfm?pageid=12372/, and "One Sneaky Clause to Look
for in Your Alarm Monitoring Contract," http://simplisafe.com/blog/one-
sneaky-clause-look-your-alarm-monitoring-contract/.

Aubrey Clark, "5 Easy Tips to Save Money on Credit Card Balance Transfers,"
Articlesbase (2008), http://www.articlesbase.com/personal-finance-articles/
5-easy-tips-for-to-save-money-on-credit-card-balance-transfers-421486.html/.

Bragg v. Linden Lab, Wikipedia: The Free Encyclopedia (2011), http://en
.wikipedia.org/wiki/Bragg_v._Linden_Lab/.

Ken LaMance, Consumer Contract Lawyers, LegalMatch (2011), www
.legalmatch.com/law-library/article/consumer-contract-lawyers/.

Christopher Elliott, "Slippery Contracts Your Customers Hate—Do You Have
One?" CBS Interactive (2011), www.bnet.com/blog/customer-management/
slippery-contracts-your-customers-hate-8212-do-you-have-one/145/.

"Everything You Need to Know about Southwest and Rapid Rewards," Wiki
FAQs (2011). http://www.southwest.com/rapidrewards/about.

Chapter 6

Stephen Dubner and Steven Levitt, "Monkey Business," *New York Times*, June 5,
2005, www.nytimes.com/2005/06/05/magazine/05FREAK.html?pagewanted=
all/.

Ned Hibberd, "How Retailers Get Shoppers to Buy More," MyFox Houston
(2010), www.myfoxhouston.com/dpp/news/consumer/100427-how-retailers-
get-shoppers-to-buy-more/ (2010).

Dan Ariely, *Predictably Irrational: The Hidden Forces that Shape Our Decisions*
(New York: HarperCollins, 2008).

Annamaria Lusardi and Olivia Mitchell, "Financial Literacy and Retirement Planning in the United States (2011), http://www.nber.org/papers/w17108/pdf/.

Angus Reed, "What Do Ontarians Think of Door-to-Door Sales?" (2009) www
.burnedatthedoor.com/survey.php/.

Ellen Shell, *Cheap: The High Cost of Discount Culture* (New York: Penguin Press,
2009).

Batsheva Ackerman, Ruslan Antonov, James Koh, Jerrad Pelkey, Jack Petty,
and Phyllis Valentine vs. the Coca Cola Company and Energy Brands. Inc.
(d/b/a Glaceau), http://health.usnews.com/health-news/blogs/on-fitness/2009/
01/15/vitaminwater-health-claim-lesson-read-labels; http://www.adweek.com/
news/advertising-branding/updated-cspi-sues-coke-over-vitaminwater-
claims-98057.

Bob Sullivan, "DirecTV Thrives on 'Deception,' Lawsuit Alleges" (2009), http://redtape.msnbc.msn.com/_news/2009/12/18/6345684-directv-thrives-on-deception-lawsuit-alleges/.

Consumer Complaints Board, "Spirit Airlines Complaints—Bogus Bait & Switch Practices!" (2011), www.complaintsboard.com/complaints/spirit-airlines-c5497.html/.

Christopher Elliott, "Spirit's Baldanza: 'The Basis for This New Fee Was Founded in Improved Customer Service'" (2010), www.elliott.org/blog/spirits-baldanza-the-basis-for-this-new-fee-was-founded-in-improved-customer-service/.

Jason Goldberg, "Top Five Takeaways: CrossView Cross-Channel Commerce Roundtable" (2011), www.crossview.com/crossview/us/galleries/images/NRF2011_FiveTakeaways.pdf.

Dean Buonomano, *Brain Bugs: How the Brain's Flaws Shape Our Lives* (New York: W.W. Norton, 2011).

On Amir, "The Pain of Deciding: Indecision, Flexibility, and Consumer Choice Online," Massachusetts Institute of Technology (unpublished thesis).

Malcolm Gladwell, *Blink: The Power of Thinking Without Thinking* (Boston: Back Bay Books, 2007).

"Consumer Conundrum: LendingTree Survey Reveals Consumers Comparison Shop for Everything Except Their Mortgage" (2007), www.freshnews.com/news/427070/consumer-conundrum-lendingtree-survey-reveals-consumers-comparison-shop-everything-exce/.

"Apathy Dominates Mobile Phone Market," M2 Presswire, October 2, 2008, http://goliath.ccnext.com/coms2/gi_0199-2103214/Apathy-dominates-mobile-phone-market.html/.

Margaret King, Philadelphia-based Center for Cultural Studies & Analysis (2010), www.culturalanalysis.com/.

Chapter 7

Dan Gillmor, "Steve Jobs Defends His PG-Rated Walled Garden" (2010), www.salon.com/technology/dan_gillmor/2010/06/02/steve_jobs_walled_garden/.

"Apple Wants 30% of Subscription Fees for Magazine, Video Apps," iPad News Daily (2011), http://www.ipadnewsdaily.com/apple-wants-30-of-subscription-fees-for-magazine-video-apps-1221/.

Marc Perton, "Apple's iTunes Pricing to Stay at 99 Cents" (2006), www.engadget.com/2006/04/21/apples-itunes-pricing-o-stay-at-99-cents/.

Jonathan Zittrain, *The Future of the Internet—and How to Stop It* (New York: Penguin Books, 2009).

Vaughan Reimers and Valerie Clulow, "The Role of Convenience in the Evolution of the Mall" (2009), www.duplication.net.au/ANZMAC09/papers/ANZMAC2009-408.pdf.

International Council of Shopping Centers, "Mall Data from ICSC: Frequently Asked Questions" (2010), www.icsc.org/srch/faq_category.php?cat_type=research&cat_id=3/.

Richard Laermer, *Punk Marketing: Get Off Your Ass and Join the Revolution* (New York: HarperCollins, 2009).

"T.J. Maxx Data Theft Worse Than First Reported," AP Story (2007), www.msnbc.msn.com/id/17853440/ns/technology_and_science-security/t/tj-maxx-data-theft-worse-first-reported/.

David Carnoy, "As iFlow Reader App Closes, Harsh Words for Apple" (2011), http://news.cnet.com/as-iflow-reader-app-closes-harsh-words-for-apple/8301-17938_105-20061802-1.html/.

The Phrase Finder (2010), www.phrases.org.uk/meanings/106700.html/.

Jacqueline Kacen and Julie Ann Lee, "The Influence of Culture on Consumer Impulsive Buying Behavior," Stanford Center on Longevity—Research Center on the Prevention of Financial Fraud (2002), www.rcpff.org/2011/02/the-influence-of-culture-on-consumer-impulsive-buying-behavior/.

Tony Dokoupil, "Is The Mall Dead?" *Newsweek*, November 12, 2008, www.newsweek.com/2008/11/11/is-the-mall-dead.html/.

Chapter 8

P. Ling, "Loyalty Rewards Valued at $48B, Travel & Hospitality No. 2 Industry" (2011), http://travel-industry.uptake.com/blog/2011/05/04/2011-colloquy-loyalty-census-48b-in-annual-rewards-points-and-miles/; CMO Council, "Getting a Business Lift from Loyalty" (2009), http://loyalty leaders.org/facts.php?catChoice=cat2.

Barbara Mikkelson, "Pudding on the Ritz" (2011), www.snopes.com/business/deals/pudding.asp/.

American Airlines, "Terms and Conditions," June 1, 2011, www.aa.com/i18n/utility/mileageExpiration.jsp/.

Greg Dragon, "AMC MovieWatcher Becomes AMC Stubs: Rewards for Money Spent versus Movies Watched" (2011), http://spicymoviedogs.com/2380/amc-moviewatcher%C2%AE-becomes-amc-stubs%E2%84%A2.html/.

"Loyalty Marketing History," Wikipedia: The Free Encyclopedia (2011), http://en.wikipedia.org/wiki/Loyalty_marketing/.

Eric Lundquist, "Harrahs Bets on IT" (2005), www.eweek.com/c/a/IT-Management/Harrahs-Bets-on-IT/.

Marguerite Rigoglioso, "Loyalty Programs Can Be a Waste of Money," Stanford Graduate School of Business (2006), www.gsb.stanford.edu/news/research/mktg_viard_rewards.shtml/.

Chapter 9

Samantha Braverman, "Most Americans Not Willing to Pay to Read News Content Online," Harris Interactive (2011), www.harrisinteractive.com/NewsRoom/HarrisPolls/tabid/447/ctl/ReadCustom%20Default/mid/1508/ArticleId/765/Default.aspx/.

"Most Read Good Morning America Stories of 2010 on ABCNews.com" (2010), http://abcnews.go.com/GMA/good-morning-america-popular-stories-2010/story?id=12499925/.

James Rainey, "On the Media: Onetime TV Consumer Watchdogs Now Ply Their Trade Elsewhere," *Los Angeles Times*, October 6, 2010, http://articles.latimes.com/2010/oct/06/entertainment/la-et-onthemedia-20101006/.

Tom Jicha, "NBC News President Steps Down" (1993), http://articles.sun-sentinel.com/1993-03-03/features/9301130057_1_michael-gartner-deborah-norville-dateline-nbc/.

Jim Fitzgerald, "Even *Consumer Reports* Fallible As Retraction on Car Seats Shows," *Insurance Journal*, January 23, 2007, www.insurancejournal.com/news/national/2007/01/23/76107.htm/.

Chapter 10

Philip Graves, *Consumer.ology: The Market Research Myth, the Truth about Consumers and the Psychology of Shopping* (Nicholas Brealey Publishing, London 2010).

"American Advertising in the American Media," DMNews magazine, December 22, 1997, http://answers.google.com/answers/threadview?id=56750/.

Jennifer Laidlaw, "Online Advertising Outstrip Newspapers" (2011), http://www.tabletedia.com/news/3691.html/.

Paul Bond, "Online Ad Revenues Hit Record High in 2010," *Hollywood Reporter* (2011), www.hollywoodreporter.com/news/online-ad-revenues-hit-record-178055/.

"14 Percent of Spam Recipients Actually Read Them?" (2009), www.dslreports.com/forum/r12570054-14-percent-of-spam-recipients-actually-read-them-/.

Pingdom, "Internet Numbers in 2010" (2010), http://royal.pingdom.com/2011/
01/12/internet-2010-in-numbers/; "Internet Numbers in 2009," http://royal
.pingdom.com/2010/01/22/internet-2009-in-numbers/; "Internet Numbers in
2008," http://royal.pingdom.com/2009/01/22/internet-2008-in-num bers/.

Tammy Worth, "Too Many Choices Can Tax the Brain, Research Shows," *Los
Angeles Times*, March 16, 2009, http://articles.latimes.com/2009/mar/16/
health/he-choices16/2/.

"Starbucks: The Numbers Guy—Starbucks Stays Mum on Drink Math," Carl
Bialik, April 2, 2008, http://blogs.wsj.com/numbersguy/starbucks-stays-mum-
on-drink-math-309/.

D. Houser, D. Reiley, and M. Urbancic, "Checking Out Temptation: A Natural
Experiment with Purchases at the Grocery Register" (2004), http://ideas
.repec.org/s/gms/wpaper.html/.

News America Marketing, "SmartSource Coupon Machine" (2011), www
.newsamerica.com/ourproducts/consumersinstore/Pages/couponmachine.aspx/.

Chapter 11

Lawrence Melton, "43% of Investors Are Easily Deceived by Investment
Scams, Finds Survey," About Broker Fraud Blog (2007), http://www
.aboutbrokerfraud.com/2007/05/43_of_investors.html/.

"Open to Exploitation: American Shoppers Online and Offline," Annenberg
Public Policy Center (2005), www.annenbergpublicpolicycenter.org/News
Details.aspx?myId=31/.

Christopher Elliott, "4 Unbelievably Stupid Things No Customer Should Ever
Do" (2011), http://onyoursi.de/2011/05/4-unbelievably-stupid-things-no-
customer-should-do/; Christopher Elliott, "Caught on Tape: Customers Who
Left Their Brains at Home" (2011), http://onyoursi.de/2011/01/caught-on-
tape-customers-who-left-their-brains-at-home/.

"Hong Kong Woman Freaks Out in Airport After Missing Flight," Reuters
.com, *New York Post*, February 16, 2009, www.nypost.com/p/news/interna-
tional/item_ExrmgiAlccCsRGIDInYRwO/.

4-Traders, "Capital One Finance: America's 'Financial IQ' Survey Shows Both
Understanding and Gaps" (2009), www.4-traders.com/CAP1-FINL-12144/
news/CAPITAL-ONE-FINANC-America-s-Financial-IQ-Survey-Shows-
Both-Understanding-and-Gaps-13159990/?imprimer=1"ca.

CFA, "Consumers Lack Knowledge of Upcoming Credit Card Protections but
are Taking Action to Protect Themselves from Recent Card Changes,

According to New Survey" (2009), www.consumerfed.org/financial-services/credit-and-debt/credit-cards/.

Glenbrook Partners, "MasterCard Survey: "'Tis the Season of the Smart Shopper," Glenbrook eCommerce Market Analysis Reports (2008), www.paymentsnews.com/2008/11/mastercard-surv.html/.

Chapter 12

Federal Trade Commission, "FTC Releases Consumer Fraud Survey" (2007), www.ftc.gov/opa/2007/10/fraud.shtm/.

Consumer Complaints Board, "GlobalCruisesOnSale.com Complaints" (2011), www.complaintsboard.com/byurl/globalcruisesonsale.com.html/.

Christopher Elliott, "How to Spot a Scam: 7 Questions to Ask Before Buying," MintLife (2011), www.mint.com/blog/consumer-iq/how-to-spot-a-scam-7-questions-to-ask-before-buying/.

Christopher Elliott, "10 Industries with the Worst Customer Service," The American Customer Satisfaction Index (2011), www.bnet.com/blog/customer-management/10-industries-with-the-worst-customer-service/626/.

Lisa Ann Schreier, *Timeshare Vacations For Dummies* (For Dummies Publishers, 2005).

Chapter 13

Audio Images, "Statistics of Message on Hold" (2010), www.mohaudio.com/Statistics-Message-on-hold.html; "Just the Facts (on Hold Marketing)", OnHold Company (2010), www.onholdcompany.com/facts.html/.

Christopher Elliott, "10 Companies that Don't Keep You Waiting On Hold Forever," CBS Interactive (2011), www.bnet.com/blog/customer-management/10-companies-that-don-8217t-keep-you-waiting-on-hold-forever/519?tag=content;drawer-container/.

Christopher Elliott, "What's a Promise Worth?," CBS Interactive (2011), www.bnet.com/blog/customer-management/whats-a-promise-worth/673/.

Christopher Elliott, "Companies That Put You 'On Hold' the Longest," CBS Interactive (2011), www.bnet.com/blog/customer-management/companies-that-put-you-on-hold-the-longest/693/.

ABC/Action News, "Woman Says She Spent 12 Hours On Hold" (2010), www.abcactionnews.com/dpp/entertainment/weird_news/woman-says-she-spent-12-hours-on-hold1284691848791WEWS-/.

Kerry Bodine, "Worst Online Chat Ever!" Kerry Bodine's Blog (2010), http://blogs.forrester.com/kerry_bodine/10-12-03-worst_online_chat_ever/.

Christopher Elliott, "Do You Know How to Serve Customer 2.0?" CBS Interactive (2011), www.bnet.com/blog/customer-management/do-you-know-how-to-serve-customer-20/639/.

Chapter 14

Monty Python's Flying Circus, Season 1, Episode 8 (2011), www.ovguide.com/tv_season/monty-pythons-flying-circus-season-1-75853.

M. Michelsen Jr., "Turning Complaints into Cash," American Salesman Journal (March 1999), www.allbusiness.com/marketing-advertising/affinity-marketing/699496-1.html/.

"Facts for Consumers: Fair Credit Billing Act," Federal Trade Commission (2009), www.ftc.gov/bcp/edu/pubs/consumer/credit/cre16.shtm/.

Epilogue

"The Cooling–Off Rule: When and How to Cancel a Sale," Federal Trade Commission (2009), www.ftc.gov/bcp/edu/pubs/consumer/products/pro03.shtm/.

"W.T. Grant: 14 Bad Business Moves that Sank the Ship," The Rat Race.com, www.businessadministration.org/blog/14-bad-business-moves-that-sank-the-ship/.

Rob Lovitt, "Fees, Fares, and the Future of Air Travel," Travel news on MSNBC.com (2010), www.msnbc.msn.com/id/40757434/ns/travel-news/t/fees-fares-future-air-travel/.

"Air Travel Consumer Report," U.S. Department of Transportation (2011), http://airconsumer.ost.dot.gov/reports/2011/February/2011FebruaryATCR.PDF/.

Max Clarke, "Informing Consumers Will Stimulate UK Economy" (2011), www.freshbusinessthinking.com/news.php?NID=8115&Title=Informing+consumers+will+stimulate+UK+economy/.

Suggested Readings

Agent Smith. "Never Send a Human to Do a Machine's Job." *The Matrix.* Warner Brothers, 1999. www.imdb.com/title/tt0133093/quotes/.

Ariely, Dan. *Predictably Irrational: The Hidden Forces that Shape Our Decisions.* Harper Perennial, 2008.

Aristotle. "What Lies in Our Power to Do, It Lies in Our Power Not to Do." www.quotes.net/quote/1841/.

Bailey, Philip James. "The First and Worst of All Frauds Is to Cheat Oneself." http://thinkexist.com/quotation/the_first_and_worst_of_all_frauds_is_to_cheat/186280.html/.

Bulwer-Lytton, Edward. "The Easiest Person to Deceive Is One's Self." www.great-quotes.com/quote/1134695/.

Bunty Bhagwan Shree Rajneesh. "The World Is Not a Problem; the Problem Is Your Unawareness." www.finestquotes.com/author_quotes-author-Bhagwan%20Shree%20Rajneesh-page-0.htm.

Buonomano, Dean. *Brain Bugs: How the Brain's Flaws Shape Our Lives.* New York: W.W. Norton and Company, 2011.

Churchill, Winston. "Never Give in Except to Convictions of Honor and Good Sense." 1941. www.winstonchurchill.org/learn/speeches/speeches-of-winston-churchill/103-never-give-in/.

Churchill, Winston. "If You Have Ten Thousand Regulations You Destroy All Respect for the Law." www.englishforums.com/English/SirWinstonChurchillThousand/lnczv/post.htm/.

Coteanu, Cristina. *Cyber Consumer Law and Unfair Trading Practices: Unfair Commercial Practices (Markets and the Law)*. Ashgate Publishing, 2005.

Erasmus, Desiderius. "Man's Mind Is So Formed That It Is Far More Susceptible to Falsehood Than to Truth." www.1-famous-quotes.com/quote/232333/.

Ford, Henry. "Don't Find Fault, Find a Remedy." www.goodreads.com/quotes/show/59811/.

Gladwell, Malcolm. *Blink: The Power of Thinking Without Thinking*. Boston: Back Bay Books, 2007.

Graves, Philip. *Consumer.ology: The Market Research Myth, The Truth about Consumers and the Psychology of Shopping*. Nicholas Brealey Publishing, 2010.

Lewis, C.S. "If You Look for Truth, You May Find Comfort in the End; If You Look for Comfort You Will Not Get Either Comfort or Truth, Only Soft Soap and Wishful Thinking to Begin, and in the End, Despair." http://www.quotedb.com/quotes/362/.

Martin, Dean. "Please Don't Talk About Me When I'm Gone." 1957. www.lyricsbox.com/dean-martin-album-this-time-im-swingin-pretty-baby-xzw24b.html/.

Montalvo, Juan. "There Is Nothing Harder than the Softness of Indifference." www.englishforums.com/English/JuanMontalvoNothingHarder/lmqxq/post.htm/.

Plato. "Whatever Deceives Men Seems to Produce a Magical Enchantment." http://thinkexist.com/quotation/whatever_deceives_men_seems_to_produce_a_magical/323017.html/.

Potter, Wendell. *Deadly Spin: An Insurance Company Insider Speaks Out on How Corporate PR Is Killing Health Care and Deceiving Americans*. Bloomsbury Press, 2010.

Santayana, George. "Habit Is Stronger Than Reason." www.great-quotes.com/quote/96635/George/Santayana/action/cite/.

Shell, Ellen. *Cheap: The High Cost of Discount Culture*. New York: Penguin Press, 2009.

Acknowledgments

ALTHOUGH SCAMMED IS a completely collaborative effort, it all started with a call—several, actually—from my literary agent, Kristina Holmes. Without her persistence and guidance, this project wouldn't have gotten off the ground.

I'm ever grateful to my day job bosses—my editors at CBS Interactive (Eric Schurenberg and Pam Kruger), Mint.com (Jennifer Coogan and Aleksandra Todorova), National Geographic Traveler (Keith Bellows and Norie Quintos), Tribune Media Services (Mary Elson and Tracy Clark), and the *Washington Post* (Joe Yonan and Zofia Smartz)—for being so understanding of my frequent absences and absent-mindedness, while I toiled away on this project.

I have the support of my colleagues and friends to thank for helping move *Scammed* from proposal to manuscript. They include Charlie Leocha at the Consumer Travel Alliance, Ben Popken at the Consumerist, and MSNBC's Bob Sullivan. Several authors also made invaluable contributions by lending their expert eyes to the book and inspiring me through their own work: Joe Calloway, Daniel Diermeier, Barry Goldsmith, Philip Graves, Doug Lansky, Chris McGinnis, Raul Pupo, and Guy Winch.

Even with all of this help, *Scammed* would have never been published were it not for the marketing insights of Jasmine Bina, the editing magic of Brent Bowers, the legal expertise of Timothy Cornell at Perry, Krumsiek & Jack, the rewriting genius of Richard Laermer, the stylings of grammar guru Char James-Tanny, and the publishing industry wisdom of Herb Schaffner.

A special thanks to my friends at John Wiley & Sons—Lauren Murphy and Christine Moore—for taking a chance on this project and seeing it through to the end.

Of course, I'd still be contemplating this book if it weren't for my better half, Kari Haugeto (thanks for the push, dear). And I wouldn't even *exist* as a consumer advocate if it weren't for the endless support of my readers and friends, particularly the ones who cheered me on via Facebook and Twitter as I wrote this in 2011, especially during those rainy June afternoons when it seemed the book would never happen.

Well, you *made* it happen. Thank you.

About the Author

Christopher Elliott is a *National Geographic Traveler* magazine's reader advocate and a nationally syndicated columnist through Tribune Media Services, which distributes his columns to the *San Francisco Chronicle*, *Chicago Tribune*, and *Philadelphia Inquirer*, among others. He writes a column for the *Washington Post* and is a personal finance columnist for Mint.com. He's the co-founder of the Consumer Travel Alliance, a Washington-based advocacy group for travelers and the current curator of On Your Side (www.onyoursi.de) a wiki and blog about customer service. He also blogs every day at Elliott.org (www.elliott.org).

Elliott is a 1990 graduate of the University of California at Irvine, where he majored in Humanities and minored in anticorporate rhetoric. He completed his Master of Journalism degree in 1991 at the University of California at Berkeley and was awarded a Fulbright Scholarship in 1996.

If you have a problem with a business—any problem—you can ping him at elliottc@gmail.com or ring him at (202) 370-7934.